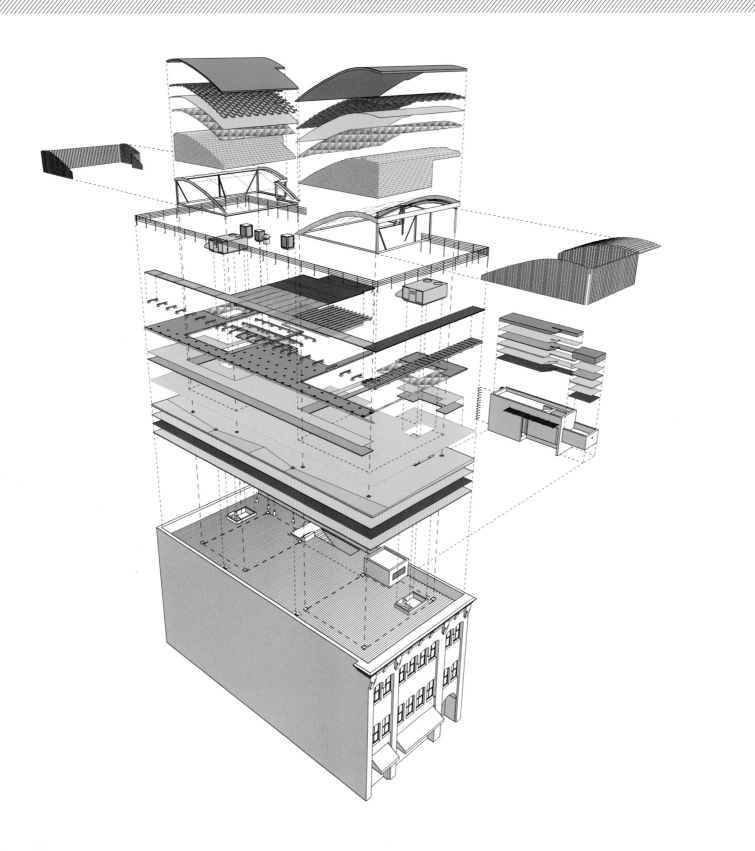

Green Roof— A Case Study

MICHAEL VAN VALKENBURGH ASSOCIATES' DESIGN

FOR THE HEADQUARTERS OF

THE AMERICAN SOCIETY OF LANDSCAPE ARCHITECTS

Christian Werthmann

PRINCETON ARCHITECTURAL PRESS, NEW YORK

Published by
Princeton Architectural Press
37 East Seventh Street
New York, New York 10003

For a free catalog of books, call 1-800-722-6657
Visit our web site at www.papress.com.

Editing: Sara Hart and Jennifer Thompson
Design: Paul Wagner

Special thanks to: Nettie Aljian, Sara Bader,
Dorothy Ball, Nicola Bednarek, Janet Behning,
Becca Casbon, Penny (Yuen Pik) Chu,
Russell Fernandez, Pete Fitzpatrick, Wendy Fuller,
Jan Haux, Clare Jacobson, John King, Nancy Eklund
Later, Linda Lee, Katharine Myers, Lauren Nelson
Packard, Arnoud Verhaeghe, Joseph Weston,
and Deb Wood of Princeton Architectural Press
—Kevin C. Lippert, publisher

Library of Congress Cataloging-in-Publication Data

Werthmann, Christian, 1964–.
Green roof : a case study / Christian Werthman.—1st ed.
    p.   cm.
"Design by Michael Van Valkenburgh Associates for the headquarters
 of the American Society of Landscape Architects."
 Includes bibliographical references.
 ISBN-13: 978-1-56898-685-2 (alk. paper)
 ISBN-10: 1-56898-685-8 (alk. paper)
 1. Green roofs (Gardening) 2. Green roofs (Gardening)—
 Washington (D.C.)—Case studies. I. Michael Van Valkenburgh
 Associates. II. Title.

 SB419.5.W47 2007
 635.9'671—dc22

                                2007004171

CONTENTS

INTRODUCTION

The topic of green roofs is closely connected to "ecological correctness," and is part of the indemnification vocabulary for sins committed in bad conscience like landscape consumption and the displacement of nature. A whole host of arguments rise from this subject, one that has been explored since the 1970s, especially in Europe. Examples of the private and public sector probably are numbered in the thousands and the professional literature of the why and how of green roof design has long been left behind and replaced by do-it-yourself applications. Today, a talented gardener is able to green his roof with the help of a building center.

In this book, the author relies on a different train of thought: life on the cool roof of a house, the view over a parapet into the distance, the addition of a new living space that can be enjoyed at dizzying heights above the traditional level of gardens and plazas.

The answer to the question of why design a green roof draws from the vision of a Mediterranean life, where it has been commonplace to use roof tops as living space for thousands of years, long before the famous hanging gardens of Babylon were built. The real answer, however, eludes a rational argument; it cannot solely be measured in energy savings and habitat for flora and fauna and cannot solely be justified through water management or compensation for lost space on the ground. The author connects to a different tradition—the modernist vision of a vertical garden city, where open spaces on the ground were insufficient to fulfill the needs of its dwellers. Therefore, the roof was propagandized as a space for children, for sport, for sun bathing, etc., basically as a garden substitute on the roof of the buildings.

Then, the conflict between the alien flat roof and more traditional roof forms was carried out with a mix of ideological and technical arguments that represented the general discussion found in the wider field of architecture. For the last fifty years the flat roof (with its new possibilities of use, including the dream of the penthouse) and the sheltering, protective pitched roof (consumed by craftsmanship and regional tradition) offered plenty of material for opposing factions.

In the search for technical solutions, the rationalists always answered the question of how to build a green roof by looking at new materials and technologies, as well as the employment of new substances for roofs and soils. The opposing faction argued that flat roofs leaked and that even a child knows that a proper house has a pitched roof. This controversy, led by technical mock arguments between modernism and traditionalism, was finally ended by the rather cumbersome achievement of technical perfection. Flat roofs are in the meantime up to par even in climates with long winters and rainy summers.

To answer why build a green roof, the author postulates a clear argument for such design, despite the current high costs. He relates to the role of landscape architecture—the profession he dedicated the book to—by consequently working through the whole case study with the most intimate detail. Thus he also follows the rationalist side by answering how green roofs are successful by reporting on the new safe technologies and the many possible mistakes that can be avoided.

It becomes clear that each generation has to lead the discussion anew from their respective standpoint. They have to instigate new experiments that not only test proven grounds but also answer with fresh results how a green roof is engineered. With new and additional research there will be more ground opened up to answer the questions of why it makes sense and to make it, through its distinct benefits, a matter of course.

Peter Latz, Ampertshausen
January 2007

Part I: Essay

THE RECLAMATION OF ROOFS

I. Green Roofs, Roof Gardens, and Hybridal Conditions

Roof gardens and green roofs both belong to a type of roof that supports vegetation. In general, the planning profession draws a clear distinction between the two types. Roof gardens are installed to be accessed and enjoyed. They are more cost intensive to construct, heavy in weight with deep soil profiles (more than six inches), and maintenance intensive. In contrast, green roofs cost a fraction of a roof garden, are lightweight with thin soil profiles, and require minimal maintenance. Most green roofs are inaccessible, and they are mainly installed for environmental performance and visual improvement. Green roofs are descended from the vernacular architecture of various countries in all parts of the globe, whereas roof gardens are known as luxury items of the affluent since the famous hanging gardens of Babylon (600 B.C.).

In the beginning of the twentieth century, roof gardens experienced a renaissance through the modernist movement. The invention of the flat roof was seen as an opportunity to inhabit a new healthy outdoor space by all levels of society. At the end of the twentieth century, the green roof gained renewed relevance through environmentalism when its varied benefits were recognized as useful for alleviating problems of heavily urbanized areas. Although the U.S. was a leader in the implementation of roof gardens at the beginning of the twentieth century, Europe took the lead in developing green roofs by the end. Only in the past couple of years has the U.S. experienced an increase in the number of green roofs with the technology imported from Europe.

Following and strengthening the trend, the American Society of Landscape Architects (ASLA) decided to retrofit its Washington, D.C., headquarters with a green roof and hired the renowned landscape architecture firm, Michael Van Valkenburgh Associates (MVVA) for its design, supported by Conservation Design Forum (CDF). The original intention of the ASLA was to build a roof that serves foremost environmental purposes. During the design process, the aspect of inhabitation came into play. The built product combines qualities typical for roof gardens (accessible and enjoyable) with elements typical for green roofs (lightweight and environmentally beneficial). The cross-breeding of the separate typologies generated a roof that answers both environmental and psychological needs.

This particular crossbreed is not a new invention. Green roof experts in the German-speaking countries already identified and labeled it as a "simple intensive roof-greening" in the 1970s.[1] In England, the combination is called a "semi-extensive or semi-intensive green roof."[2] Both terms are of a strict technical nature, somewhat unsatisfying by creating the vague impression of being neither/nor. The design team for the ASLA roof frequently referred during the working process to its roof as a "Hybrid"—a title indicating a more autonomous quality. Sidestepping nomenclature, this book revolves around two questions: How important and feasible is this roof type for future roof conversions? How is the roof put together and how does it function?

As a research method an inductive approach was chosen that tries to gain wide insights through the in-depth examination of one example, the new ASLA roof.

II. The Former ASLA Roof—an HVAC Desert

In 1997, the American Society of Landscape Architects bought a three-story brownstone building in the middle of Washington, D.C. The building is situated in a block of infill development, flanked by similarly sized buildings and surrounded by a mix of two- to seven-story structures. The roof of the building measures about 82 by 35 feet and represents 2,900 square feet out of 262 million square feet of roof surface in the city.

Access to the former roof was not easy. One had to climb up a ladder in a narrow shaft, open a chain lock and push a hatch skywards, then crawl through the hatch onto the roof. Once the hatch was opened, an abrupt change of environment took place; one was immediately struck by the blinding glare of the albedo-colored waterproofing membrane that spanned over the whole roof like shark skin; even in overcast conditions, the glare was severe. Such exposure amplified the perception of the elements. The light appeared stronger, the rain hit harder, and temperature seemed to be more perceptible.

Undesigned, the utilitarian terrain was a strange but fascinating place. The "shark skin" was cushioned by an insulation layer and there was indeed the feeling of walking on something alive. Strange boxes with metal panes and grates seemed randomly dispersed over the small area of the roof, emanating a humming sound. The unobstructed 360-degree views and interesting views down to the street life were very appealing, and the connection from the roof to the street felt more immediate than just gazing out of a window.

Next to the ASLA roof, there are several other roofs similarly packed with equipment and with no signs of human occupation.

It is comforting to know that the ASLA roof has changed into an

TOP: Roof greening typology
BOTTOM: Photo-collage of the ASLA
roof before the retrofit

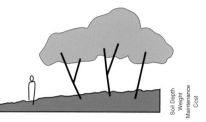

German Terminology:	Green Roof	Green Roof Hybrid	Roof Garden
	Extensive roof-greening	**Simple intensive roof-greening**	**Intensive roof-greening**
	Maintenance extensive	Maintenance extensive	Maintenance intensive
	Inaccessible	Accessible	Accessible
	Low weight	Low to medium weight	Heavy weight
	Low cost	Medium cost	High cost

PVC WATERPROOFING
INSULATION
STEEL DECKING
STEEL STRUCTURE

TOP: Back alley in New York, nicknamed "Bandit's Roost," 1887
MIDDLE: Housing barracks in New York, around 1890; children were brought onto the roof to escape the unsanitary and unsafe conditions of the ground.

BOTTOM: Dwelling on the roof in the Bruchfeldstrasse housing development in Frankfurt, 1922; staged commercial photograph with hired models, dressed in the latest fashion

accessible amenity, but it leaves one wondering why engaging spaces like this roof and the roofs next to it—in a densely packed city—were left unused to begin with?

III. The Shattered Dreams of Modernism

When going back in time, it becomes clear that the current idea of the barren roof was never intended. In the beginning of the last century, an international group of visionary architects and planners dreamed of a city whose flat roofs were crowned by roof gardens. Modern architecture, guided by the hygienic movement, reacted to the unsanitary and crowded conditions of the ninteenth-century city.

The breakthrough of flat-roof technology at the end of the nineteenth century triggered the idea to build roof gardens and terraces en masse to fulfill the demand for "light, air, and sun."[3] In 1930 the German landscape architect Harry Maasz predicted a metropolis where "man will stroll from roof garden to roof garden which will continuously crown the tops of our cities as sunlit and flowering paradises."[4] Le Corbusier, the mastermind of the movement, heroically proclaimed "the conquest of the flat roof"[5] and incorporated the roof garden as one of his five elements toward a new architecture. He promised the fulfillment of an age old dream: "to climb on one's roof."[6]

It was an act of emancipation. The entrance to the new outdoor space was intended for everybody, not only for dukes, kings, and millionaires as in the centuries before.

Prototypes of inhabitable roofs were erected on an urban level: the Weissenhofsiedlung in Stuttgart (1927), the residential areas of the new Frankfurt of Ernst May (1927) and the Rockefeller Center in New York (1930). In 1952 Le Corbusier built his famous Unité d'Habitation, the irrefutable icon of an inhabitable roof.[7]

In the following fifty years, architects integrated inhabitable rooftops and terraces into their designs. A fair number of roof gardens were built and many residential structures were designed as terrace buildings.[8] The inhabitable roof gained a firm position in the everyday vocabulary of the profession, and landscape architects learned to deal with "on-structure" conditions on an every day basis. However, today the majority of rooftops in the U.S. are still deserted.

In the downtown of a dense city like Boston, only a few roofs are inhabited, the majority are given over to technical equipment, or as the architect Joseph MacDonald has put it: "Today the roof is in the firm hands of the HVAC guys."[9] Technology from inside the building has taken over the outside. Air handlers, ventilation pipes, window-washing equipment, and heating vents pop up as the floor plan below commands. The rest is waterproofing. What happened to the promised proliferation of roof gardens?

In Boston, one might blame it on the severe climate, but the presence of roof gardens is less dependent on climate issues as one might assume.[10] In a dense and affluent neighborhood like Commonwealth Avenue in Boston, almost every roof is in use and has some form of a terrace.

If roof-top use remains a privilege of the wealthy living in historic districts, the democratic promise of the modern movement to build roof gardens for everybody has obviously failed.

Thereby a variety of factors played a role. The biggest factor was and is the considerable additional expense of a roof garden compared to a regular roof. One must not forget that the flat roof is attractive to a developer because it is less costly than a sloped roof. The addition of a roof garden eradicates those savings. It is not only the additional cost of the garden that has to be paid for but also the reinforcement of the whole structure that has to hold the weight of the garden. There is also a considerable financial commitment to maintaining a garden that is mostly out of sight from social supervision. For the average developer who has a revenue expectation of seven years, the increase in value of the property through a roof garden does not occur fast enough to be profitable, moving the roof garden into the realm of a luxury item.

Other factors had considerable influence as well, like the exodus of the middle class into low-density suburbs that drained the city of people who could have asked for and afforded a condensed architecture of roof gardens and terraces. On top of this, technical shortcomings like the leakage problems of early roof gardens created an aura of suspicion and avoidance—prejudices that persist up to today. Finally, it has to be acknowledged that a majority of buildings do not have the programmatic need for intensive roof gardens, such as industrial buildings, warehouses, most commercial buildings, and residences in low-density areas with too low a population to profit from a roof garden or with too much open space around.

About thirty years ago, the desolate sight of these bare flat roofs triggered a counter movement in the German-speaking countries of Europe. Methods of exchanging the gravel of ballast roofs for a thin coat (three

TOP: Downtown Boston

BOTTOM: In the dense living quarters around Commonwealth Avenue in Boston (five- to six-story-tall blocks), roofs account for more than one third of the total outdoor space available. In this affluent neighborhood, almost every building has some sort of roof terrace.

Commonwealth Avenue

Standard Roof   Parking   Terrace   Garden

0   500 ft

to five inches) of growing medium were tested. The low weight of the soil made structural reinforcement of the existing roofs unnecessary, thus substantially reducing costs. They also found that the minimal type of a "roof greening" (the direct translation from the German) provided similar environmental benefits as a traditional roof garden. The thin coatings retained and cleaned rain water, cooled and humidified the surrounding air, filtered dust, reduced noise levels, insulated against heat, provided habitat for flora and fauna, and prolonged the life expectancy of the roof. The technology was widely implemented as a remedy against many problems of urban density, such as frequent flooding, water and air pollution, and high energy consumption.

Since 1998 there has been a growing movement in the U.S. toward the installation of green roofs and the ASLA retrofit uses green-roof technology at its core. It is worthwhile to take a closer look at the history and current status of green roofs in Europe in order to not only better understand its origins but to better judge the quality and composition of the currently imported product.

IV. The Rise of Green Roofs

VERNACULAR PRECEDENTS

For many centuries, grass roofs have been built in northern countries like Scandinavia, Canada, and Iceland for insulation from the extreme cold. Similarly, the indigenous tribes of Tanzania cover their huts with soil as a shield against the searing heat.[11] Throughout Europe earth roofs were commonly used for their insulating effect on utilitarian structures. Wine and beer cellars were traditionally built with layers of earth to reduce temperature extremes. Already in 1860, grass roofs were propagated by the head of the building department Eduard Rüber in Munich, using similar arguments that green roof proponents use today.[12]

EARLY GREEN ROOF PIONEERS

Although much cited today, the vernacular examples of northern countries and the studies of Rüber did not trigger the German green roof movement. There were "unintentional" green roofs in Germany that raised the curiosity of some researchers. These roofs, built around 1900, consisted of wood construction overlaid with tar-board. For fire prevention, the tar-board was covered with a thin layer of sand and gravel. Over the years, the soil mix naturally attracted a layer of spontaneous vegetation. Reinhard Bornkamm, a botanist in Göttingen, had a view from his

office over one of these grass roofs while writing his dissertation, inspiring him to make the vegetation of these roofs the topic of his next study. In 1957 he published a paper with a botanical analysis of thirty-seven vegetated roofs he found in the region.[13]

While Bornkamm at that time was mostly curious about the botanical aspects of the plant communities, he only later recognized the importance of his studies for greening new roofs. In 1975, Bornkamm would eventually become one of the pioneers of modern green-roof design by placing and planting thin layers of soils on a gravel ballast roof at the Free University of Berlin.[14]

THE FOUNDING OF THE FLL

Contemporaneously, an influential research society for landscape development and landscape construction, the Forschungsgesellschaft Landschaftsentwicklung Landschaftsbau e.V. (FLL), was founded (1975). In 1978 a subcommittee "Vegetation technology for green spaces of residential areas" was installed for the purpose of examining vegetation on roofs.[15]

A group of twenty to thirty people consisting of horticulturalists, landscape architects, landscape contractors, and researchers regularly met and discussed the technical aspects of roof-greening. Although roof gardens played the dominant role in the beginning, the group began to discuss green roof concepts influenced by Bornkamm's studies and examples in Switzerland. The Germans labeled the new technology as "extensive roof-greening" versus "intensive roof-greening," which is associated with roof gardens. The terms "extensive" and "intensive" describe the grade of maintenance needed for a specific cultivation system and its degree of sustainability. Green roofs are considered extensive because they should require only little maintenance and be self regenerating.

From the beginning, the FLL did not only promote extensive roof-greening as an aesthetic remediation for the vast gravel areas of large flat roofs, they also recognized its ecological benefits. Hans-Joachim Liesecke, a professor emeritus for vegetation technology and one of the founding members of the subcommittee, wrote in 1975: "For the construction of extensive, basically maintenance free roof-greenings with low growing and drought tolerant plants, there are aesthetic as well as microclimatic reasons that call for an additional greening of unused gravel areas."[16]

The sign spells "Stoneham" in this twenty-year-old cartoon from Stefan Lucas, published in *Garten und Landschaft*, the main landscape architecture magazine in Germany (no. 10, 1984).

More knowledge, especially about the ecological functions of green roofs, was accumulated over the years through research programs on German universities and the experiences of landscape contractors on the roofs. At the landscape department at Kassel University, Professor Peter Latz initiated one of the first green roof research programs in the early 1980s that laid the foundation for the modern low organic and highly mineralic green roof substrates used today. In 1982 the FLL issued its first roof-greening guidelines. The basic urban, ecological, and economical arguments for green roofs that are still in use today were already outlined in this document.

THE GREEN REVOLUTION

The beginnings of green roofs in Germany originated from the green profession—horticulturalists, botanists, landscape architects, and contractors. However, the pioneering work of a small research group does not explain the extreme success and proliferation of green roofs in the German-speaking countries of Europe. Earlier attempts to build grass roofs did not turn into widespread applications (as the example of Eduard Rüber shows). The findings of the early green roof pioneers of the seventies was propelled forward by a much bigger social force—the rise of environmentalism.

Already in the late 1960s, modern architecture was violently rejected by large parts of the population in Germany. This rejection came from a counterculture that had its roots in the '68 revolution and was fed by an explosive mix of nostalgia and environmental frustration. *The Inhospitability of Cities: An Instigation to Discord* was a famous and much cited 1965 book by the psychologist Alexander Mitscherlich. Its title and content pinpoints the feelings of the time. Mitscherlich wrote in his foreword: "The sight of the growing formations, that used to be cities, proves, that they resemble a human being, who is disfigured by cancerous metastases."[17]

In 1984 the influential exhibition "Grün kaputt" (*Green kaput*) traveled through Germany. Its curators chastised the aesthetic degradation of the built environment through explicit imagery that showed the massive loss of trees, the disfigurement of traditional architecture, the anonymous facades of inferior modern buildings, and the unintelligent application of modern building materials like PVC, aluminum, and concrete. The criticism was based on aesthetics rather than ecology, with concrete transformed into a symbol for everything that was wrong.

Concrete and green were the yin and yang of their time—concrete being the evil, which had to be replaced by green. In addition to the aesthetic discontent with the built environment, came the growing awareness and disapproval of environmental outrages. The eco-movement grew in the 1980s into a broad and influential force. It was in its core anti-technical—"Back to Nature" was the famous slogan. In contrast to the U.S., the German Green Party found its way into the parliament (1983) and left a lasting impact on public policy.

In this climate, the bare roofs of modern buildings had to be camouflaged, and to be covered like the rest of the building with a "green fur." At its inception, the trigger for Germany's green roof movement was not only the prospect of ecological benefits but the deep aesthetic discontent with the status quo of the built environment. Very different from the origins of the modernist movement, the environmental revolution originated not from the design profession, but from concerned citizens and environmental activists. The roof-garden movement of the thirties was about the emancipation of man, the eco-movement of the eighties was about the emancipation of nature: a new "conquest of the roof" by plants and animals.

In summary, the environmental movement sharply increased overall sensibilities toward the ecology and aesthetic of the built environment. The research of the green roof pioneers did not stay in the realm of academia, they actually found wide acceptance by a sensitized population.

V. A Showpiece of Bioengineering

Over the years the discussion and research in Germany started to focus more on the environmental than aesthetic qualities of green roofs. German municipalities began to realize that extensive implementation of green roofs help them to better manage storm water, curb flooding, and combined sewer overflows. In the 1980s, cities like Stuttgart, which lies in a basin over a freshwater reservoir, started to mandate the new technology particularly to reduce city temperatures and ground water pollution. Today, forty municipalities all over Germany have regulations that either encourage or mandate green roof construction, and state and federal laws give various forms of incentives for implementation.

THE DEVELOPMENT OF A GREEN ROOF INDUSTRY AND ITS PRODUCTS

The mandatory implementation of green roofs spurred the formation of a green roof industry with its own research agenda. Built projects

Green roofs in Weiler Park, a new commercial district in Stuttgart; roofs appear reddish brown due to mid-summer drought.

were a rich source and influence for the development of the technology. Manufacturers responded to the special needs and budgets of their clients. Concerned building owners had to be convinced that their green roofs would not leak, be perforated, burn, blow off, clog pipes, die, or be excessively expensive to build or to maintain. Pioneering work was done by rigorously testing materials and vegetation systems.

In a thirty-year-long process, the German green roof development finally arrived at highly technical, reliable, lightweight, inexpensive, and maintenance-extensive green roof systems. The green-roof guidelines of the FLL were continuously updated and serve today as the bible for correct implementation that is adopted by other countries. The green roof industry grew into a $540 million per year enterprise—seven percent of the German roof industry.

Although numbers vary widely, an estimated total of fifty square miles of green roofs exist in Germany and an estimated 4.8 square miles of green roofs are added each year.[18] Although there are many different types of green roofs, the main bulk of these roofs consist of a thin mineral substrate (2 1/2" to 4") that is planted with one genus: sedum.

SEDUM, THE WORKHORSE OF THE INDUSTRY

Thirty years of German green roof development culminated in the dominance of one species, and it is common in the profession to equate sedum with green roofs. When I talked to a Boston-based landscape architect about my research, he said: "It's just sedum, isn't it?"

Given the many plants that can colonize roofs, the sedum=green roof equation is a gross oversimplification. But why is sedum so successful? A closer examination of the genus is revealing.

Sedum is naturally occurring in locations that bear climatic and geologic similarities to rooftop conditions. There are more than five hundred different species of sedum that grow on a wide range of soil structures like limestone, volcanic rock, loess, bare rock, and in scree, mainly in the northern hemisphere. The structure of sedum enables it to survive in arid climates. It has thick cuticles, small cells, small volume of internal airspace, large vacuoles for water storage, protected stomata, and a minimal root system. Up to ninety-five percent of the total volume of the succulent can be dedicated to water storage.

During hot days sedum has developed a special form of photosynthesis called Crassulacean acid metabolism (CAM). CAM keeps the plant's breathing pores closed during the day, opening only in the cooler

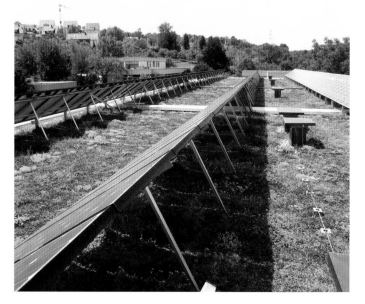

2 guard cells control opening into leaf
thickened inner walls expand + contract
stomata opening permits gases to enter + leave the leaf
nucleus
chloroplasts

fuel = CO₂

CO2 enters through open stomata into the
chlorenchyma cells, the main photosynthetic cell

2am

CO₂   50°F

CO₂

fixation by PEP carboxylase

produces malate,
a common acid in many fruits + vegetables
which is stored inside vacuoles

PEP

some CAM plants can permanently
close their stomata to prevent water loss and re-cycle the
CO₂ within the cells (known as CAM-idling) for weeks

6am

10pm

upper epidermis (mulptiple cell layers)
fewer, sunken stomata lowers
exposure to air currents
large vacuoles for water storage;
up to 95% of the total volume of
succulent plants

leaf section

temperature rise releases CO₂ into
Calvin cycle + normal photosynthesis;
open stomata also absorb
atmospheric CO₂ in cool mornings

calvin cycle

stomata
detail

6 pm

sugars

10am

night
day

110°F

2pm

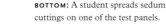

TOP: By spreading sedum on a two-inch gravel-ballast roof, the perseverance of the species is tested to the extreme. So far, half of the cuttings survived the summer of '06 without any additional watering. (Pilot study on the roof of the Graduate School of Design, Harvard University. Study designed by Christian Werthmann, Katrin Scholz-Barth, and Barbara Deutsch.)

BOTTOM: A student spreads sedum cuttings on one of the test panels.

evening to absorb carbon dioxide. The CO_2 is converted into, and stored as, malic acid. A rise in temperature the next day triggers the breakdown of the acid and release of carbon dioxide. The released CO_2 is then available for photosynthesis. CAM basically enables sedum to photosynthesize during the day without opening its pores for CO_2 intake like other plants, thereby shutting down evaporation.

In extremely arid conditions, some CAM plants can even close their stomata day and night to prevent water loss and recycle the carbon dioxide within the cells (known as CAM-idling). While this does not allow any growth, it allows for maintenance of the healthy state of the cells.

CAM works in favor of vegetation strategies using sedum in the extreme living conditions on roofs, where temperatures can vary greatly from very cold to extremely hot in a short period and water supply is unpredictable. Whereas in German climates xerophytes (plants that grow in arid conditions) are in deep soils displaced by mesophytes (plants that grow in average moisture conditions), the special architecture and metabolism of sedum gives it an edge over mesophytes on the thin and mostly mineral substrates of green roofs.

In addition to this extraordinary metabolism, sedum can be easily propagated; roots grow from fallen or severed leaves and can spread rapidly. It does not grow very high, looks orderly, and requires only a minimum amount of maintenance (no mowing needed).

With the rise of mandatory green roofs in Germany, developers have sought the most cost-effective and low-maintenance approach. Utilizing a sedum carpet is currently seen as the most economical method of compliance. When asked about the reason for the widespread sedum application, most German green roof manufacturers stress durability, extreme drought tolerance, self-propagation, ease of installation, minimal maintenance, and low costs.

A SHOWPIECE OF BIOENGINEERING

Sedum is typically planted on a sophisticated selection of materials with interdependent functions. The specification and composition of the singular components vary widely, are intensively researched, and are at the core of the success formula of each manufacturer. In generic green roof construction, the layers typically consist of a growing medium that provides nutrients and structural support for the plants, a filter fabric that prevents the growing medium from sifting through, a drainage layer that drains (and sometimes retains) excess storm water, a protection layer

Section through a generic green roof and a sedum leaf; functional similarities become apparent.

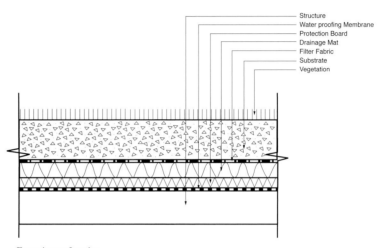

Structure
Water proofing Membrane
Protection Board
Drainage Mat
Filter Fabric
Substrate
Vegetation

Extensive roof section

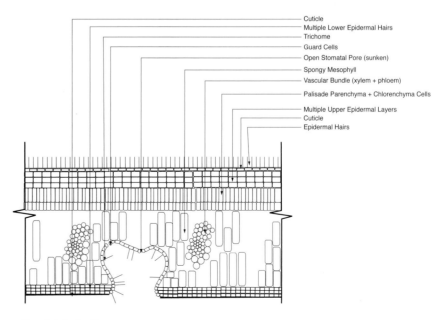

Cuticle
Multiple Lower Epidermal Hairs
Trichome
Guard Cells
Open Stomatal Pore (sunken)
Spongy Mesophyll
Vascular Bundle (xylem + phloem)
Palisade Parenchyma + Chlorenchyma Cells
Multiple Upper Epidermal Layers
Cuticle
Epidermal Hairs

Xerophyte leaf section

that protects the waterproofing from incidental perforation (it can also be the insulation), and a root-resistant waterproofing that is laid onto the structure of the building.

If one compares the section of a generic green roof with a sedum leaf section, structural similarities become apparent.

Both have waterproofing, insulation layers, storage cells, openings and filters. Both perform sophisticated functions under various climatic and seasonal conditions. Obviously sedum, with its sophisticated metabolism, executes much more complicated tasks than the materials of the roof, but the two together create a fusion between evolution and engineering. They build a living skin with specifiable performance characteristics that is fine-tuned to the artificial habitat of a roof—in short, a perfect example of the modern art of bioengineering.

Imagine that green roofs do not exist and an engineer has to invent a new roof surface; he would be overwhelmed by its performance specification: Develop a new roof material that is light (20 lb/sf), inexpensive ($5/sf), fireproof, doubles the roof life, stores rain water (fifty percent), converts carbon dioxide into oxygen, filters dust, moderates ambient temperature, dampens noise (5dB), and needs minimal maintenance (twice a year).

GREEN ROOF STASIS

The fulfillment of this specification by sedum roofs is a feat of bioengineering but also shows how much control over a biological surface already has been achieved. Flux, succession, and change—all inherent traits of landscapes on the ground—are not desired on sedum roofs. Indeed, the opposite is the case. Sedum roofs are designed to resist change. Their success is based on the delivery of a stable product that performs as per specification over a certain period of time. Green roofs need "to get a job done." And not only in an environmental sense: they are quantifiable technical surfaces that are held liable against a set of requirements outlined by the FLL. To compound matters, green roofs are part of a particularly sensitive area of the building and are exposed to special scrutiny by the German construction industry, which still perceives flat roofs as prone to water leakage. German landscape architects are under pressure and have to sign a warranty of thirty years for their green roofs. They prefer to choose systems that are known to be reliable. The widely acknowledged and industrially manufactured sedum roof systems set the standard.

PRODUCTIVE LANDSCAPES

The emphasis on performance indicates that green roofs are far from being gardens and are viewed instead as productive landscapes. Per definition, productive landscapes have to perform in a utilitarian way and are not designed to evoke differentiated emotions in humans like gardens or parks do. Green roofs that have to store a certain amount of water are not different from vineyards that have to produce a certain amount of grapes or from turf that has to sustain a certain number of football games per year.

The sedum roofs of today symbolize performance-oriented green roof design. Like fine-tuned engines, they run on leaner artificial substrates with almost no organic content; volcanic rock or expanded shale, baked at 2000° Fahrenheit, make the substrates lighter and soil depths as thin as possible. They seem to be race cars in the fleet of green roofs—maximum performance paired with minimum weight. The simple soil mixtures and roof sections of the early days developed into multilayered complex systems supporting the homogenous surface of succulents. The unkempt and rough gave way to the groomed and cultivated, reminiscent of the unrelenting beauty of agricultural fields.

GROWN UP?

The modern sedum roofs do not seem to belong to the generation of environmental activists that tried to change the world thirty years ago; they instead belong to a technically savvy society, which cultivates high-tech products like performance fleece, PowerBars, and carbon-fiber bicycles. As the German eco-movement has come of age, green roofs have grown up as well (with all the advantages and disadvantages of adulthood). The current technical focus stands in contrast to the 1970s "Back to Nature" mandate that was necessary to spearhead the movement, but had to be overcome for it to enter mainstream architecture. Today, modern green roof technology is far removed from any eco-romance or political ideology.

VI. Roofs for Biodiversity

The proliferation of sedum carpets is not unanimously approved, and has raised some concern. Its critics point out that the mandatory implementation of green roofs in Europe has led to low-cost and low-quality sedum roofs with reduced ecological and environmental performance capacities.

TOP LEFT: Spontaneously colonized roof in Berlin, 1981; Canada Bluegrass dominates.

BOTTOM LEFT: Soil of a roof supporting herbaceous vegetation

TOP RIGHT: Green roof of a congress center in Basel, 2005; sedum species dominate.

BOTTOM RIGHT: Lightweight aggregate growing medium with low organic content supporting drought-tolerant succulents

TOP: Local soils that mimic former riverbank conditions were placed on the roof of the Rossetti building in Basel.

BOTTOM: The ninety-year-old Moos water filtration plant supports a nine-acre roof meadow with a sizable community of green-winged orchids.

Stephan Brenneisen, a Swiss green roof specialist and ecologist, claims that many of the thin substrates on sedum roofs lose their effectiveness over time. Some of the used substrates tend to become acidic and do not sufficiently provide minerals and nutrients for the long-term health of the sedum plants. Owners rarely fertilize their sedum roofs on a regular basis and the plants suffer after a couple of years. Brenneisen also found that many sedum roofs have minimal positive effects on storm water retention, energy use, or the urban climate—core arguments that have been used to justify the implementation of green roofs.[19] Moreover, ecologists attribute rather limited biodiversity values to sedum roofs and prefer roofs that offer a secondary habitat to endangered plant and animal species.

For example, Brenneisen created a 16,000-square-foot green roof on top of a new hospital building in Basel, designed by one of today's leading architectural firms, Herzog & de Meuron. He likes to deviate from the thin and lean artificial substrates of the industry toward thicker (more than three inches) and richer soils that mimic local site conditions. The flat roof of the seven-year-old Rossetti building is coated with a substrate that varies in thickness from three inches to small hills of fifteen-inch depth. The soil consists of a sandy to loamy gravel taken from the region. Compared to the lightweight soil compositions used by the industry, Brenneisen's mix seems old-fashioned and underdesigned. However, the soil was highly successful for habitat creation. Six years after the roof was seeded with a mix of local grassland plants, a colony of rare spiders and fifty-two beetle species have been found. The building is close to the river Rhine in Basel, and some of the species found on this roof are typical inhabitants of river banks.

Brenneisen ascribes the roof's success to the fact that he used local materials for the substrate and that the varying soil thickness enabled a richer plant and animal life. The small mounds enable insects to survive the winter, whereas they would freeze to death in thinner substrates.

MOOS WATER FILTRATION PLANT

Brenneisen believes that his roofs will get richer in biodiversity over the years. He likes to show the potential long-range benefits of his designs by referring to a green roof in Zürich that is now ninety years in service.

The lake water filtration plant Moos built in 1914 was a product of engineering excellence of the time. Water from the lake of Zürich is pumped into the building and is cleaned to drinking-water quality as it slowly filters through a layer of sand. It was the first reinforced concrete building in Zürich and was outfitted with a nine-acre earth roof for temperature moderation (following a longstanding European tradition of using earth roofs for cooling purposes).

During its ninety-year lifespan, the roof had to be reworked only on its edges; the rest of the waterproofing remained functional.

The three-inch-thick concrete ceiling is sealed with a three-quarter-inch mastic asphalt membrane and then overlaid with six to eight inches of topsoil. The goal was to prevent the lake water from overheating in the summer and freezing over in winter. Presumably the soil on the roof came from or near the construction site and was not seeded. Today, the roof supports a stable meadow community with 175 different plant species and six thousand specimens of a rare orchid.[20] Many plants are on the endangered or rare species list of Switzerland.

The high biodiversity is attributed to the fact that the soil layer is deep enough to sustain a meadow and that the area was not exposed to the typical disturbances of sites on the ground, like foot traffic, surface run-off, grazing, pesticides, or fertilization. The soil that was placed on the roof acted like a seed bank of regional plant species. The rest of the plant community came through seed dispersion by birds, ants, and wind. For the past thirty years (and presumably before), the meadow has been mown twice per year (July and October), with the clippings being removed.

The plant ecologist Elias Landolt, who surveyed the flora of the roof, stated that the meadow "reflects the species richness of an agricultural region at the beginning of the twentieth century."[21] The protected location on the roof and the continuous maintenance regime of the meadow preserved a plant community that does not exist on the ground anymore. Landolt motioned to put the roof under a cantonal (state level) preservation status. Who of the original civil engineers would have guessed that?

GREEN ROOF REGIONALISM?

Striking examples like the Moos plant provoke ecologists to claim that unused roofscapes of modern buildings ought to be used for conservation purposes. Brenneisen states that "there is no other comparable area type in urban spaces with so little competition for its use." He later continues: "If rooftop space is not used by the occupiers of a building, it can be returned to nature."[22] The fundamental idea that green roofs

TOP: The roof of Corbusier's Petite Maison was an accessible green roof.
BOTTOM: The uppermost roof of the La Tourette monastery is a landscape for strolling and meditation, an early hybrid between green roof and roof garden.

Atelier 5 followed Corbusier's example and covered all roofs of the experimental Halen housing project with 4 to 6 inches of soil, 1958.

(even on their artificial location) are treated as dynamic landscapes reflecting the climate and location of a region is intriguing. Especially in the United States, the many different climate zones and rich plant palette offer a large research field for suitable roof-plant communities. Several American universities currently test indigenous plants that occur in roof-like conditions like in scree or talus. The first results though are mixed. When it comes to suitable plant selections for thin and light-weight substrates on roofs that have very limited load bearings, sedum still outperforms many native plants as a reliable base cover in the hotter and longer summers of the temperate climate zones in North America.[23] Outside those temperate zones, like in the tropical South or in the arid landscapes of the West, reliable plant material has still to be found.

Besides suitable plant selections, a different question surfaces. Is society ready for green roofs that are characterized by flux, succession, and death? The Swiss with their long-standing tradition of inserting the "wild" into the middle of their meticulously clean cities might accept the "unkempt" look of Brenneisen's roofs, yet similar concepts like Paul Kephart's native grass design for the large new roof of the California Academy of Sciences in San Francisco (currently in construction) were rejected. The brown color of the cool-season grasses at their summer dormancy was not acceptable for the client.[24]

VII. Unused Precedents

The current discussion about the roofs for biodiversity sheds new light onto the historic work of a modernist icon. Le Corbusier not only propagated the idea of inhabitable gray roofs, like at the Unité d'Habitation, he also built green roofs that bear similarities to the discussed examples in Switzerland. Corbusier typically used soils found on site and placed them without much horticultural treatment (no soil amendment, seeding, or planting) on his roofs—relying on spontaneous plant colonization.[25] Already in 1923 he completed a house for his parents with a ten-inch-deep earth roof.[26]

Whereas Petite Maison can be seen as an early example for a mix between a roof garden and a green roof, the monastery Sainte Marie de la Tourette, finished forty years later in 1960, has both—inaccessible and accessible green roofs.

All flat and sloped roofs of the monastery are overlaid with a thin layer (four inches) of soil. The accessible areas are situated over the outer ring and are designed for strolling and meditation. This hybrid is framed by a five-foot-high parapet concentrating the views inside toward the sculpted ventilation shafts.

The grass roofs of the ambulatory, the two chapels, and the vestry are pure green roofs; they are inaccessible and only visible from above. These lower roofs are formed as elegant trays for the soil. A slightly upturned concrete wall retains four inches of earth, barely sufficient for the survival of drought-tolerant herbs and grasses. The balance between the volumes of the courtyard buildings, the thickness of the walls, and the size of the grass rectangles is perfect and timeless.

In La Tourette Le Corbusier mastered the unprecedented integration of green roof technology into a spiritual *Gesamtkunstwerk*. Tragically, Le Corbusier's green roof examples did not find their way into the mainstream vocabulary of modern architecture. Although roof terraces and gardens were built by many architects, Le Corbusier's earth roofs were not copied.

Only a group of young Swiss architects, ardent admirers of Le Corbusier's work, truthfully followed his footsteps and even superceded him in the practice of constructing green roofs. With their groundbreaking housing project, Halen, finished in 1958, Atelier 5 orchestrated the most extensive implementation of earth roofs at the same time as Corbusier's monastery was built.

VIII. The ASLA Roof—Between Green Roof and Roof Garden

As outlined, there are various trajectories and developments in the past and contemporary world of vegetated roofs. Early in the last century the social and sanitary movement propagated the use of roofs as a reaction to the unhealthy and dim conditions of the dense nineteenth-century city. Those ideas were later incorporated into the vocabulary of modern architecture, resulting in roof gardens, terrace houses, and roof terraces that were mostly paved and kept vegetation in little planters.[27] In Europe the rise of environmentalism in the 1970s provided fertile ground for turning grey into green roofs mainly for ecological and visual reasons. The emotional "Back to Nature" movement developed into the performance-oriented phase of today, which seeks to build efficient green infrastructure without much concern for social accessibility.

One has to keep this trajectory in mind when analyzing a project like the ASLA roof. The mere fact that green-roof technology is employed does not make this roof stand out from other green roofs. From a European perspective, its environmental benefits are old news. It was obvious that lightweight green-roof technology had to be applied if something were to grow on a roof that was not designed to support much more than its own weight.

The ASLA roof's real contribution is how its design goes beyond environmental performance. It was not about developing a generic green roof carpet, it meant to explore the cultural, aesthetic, and experiential potential of green roof technology in order to transform a roof desert into a pleasant and engaging outdoor space that can be accessed and enjoyed on a daily basis. Classical design considerations like material selection, spatial and sculptural formation, entrance sequencing, view creation, context manipulation, tactility, vegetation experiences, and microclimatic conditioning played essential roles in shaping the outcome. The real innovation of the ASLA roof design lies in the fusion of the environmental with the humane. This fusion can be best exemplified on two design elements—the "waves" and the grating.

THE WAVES

The two vegetated waves, as the most prominent elements on the roof, create an artificial topography that sets up new relationships between the visitor of the roof and the surrounding city.

The waves, filled with lightweight foam overlaid by a thin layer of substrate, achieved the desirable quality of an object that performs several functions at once. By framing the deck, the waves embed the visitor in the roof, provide shelter from wind, create an artificial horizon directing and blocking views, indicate the green transformation of the roof from street level, hide mechanical units, and showcase vegetation while still fulfilling all the typical ecological functions of a generic green roof. The invention of multifunctional elements like the waves is key in situations where there is only limited space available. However the greatest merit of the tectonic manipulation is its transformation of a generic green roof carpet into a sensual garden.

Thereby the designers followed a behavior pattern of landscape architects from the past, who brought elements of productive landscapes into garden design. The formal bosque of trees in French gardens can be derived from the regular tree rows of orchards or logging forests. The English lawn is the cultivated version of a meadow. In this case, the sedum carpet is transformed from a flat plane into a tectonic object that creates a hospitable space for human beings.

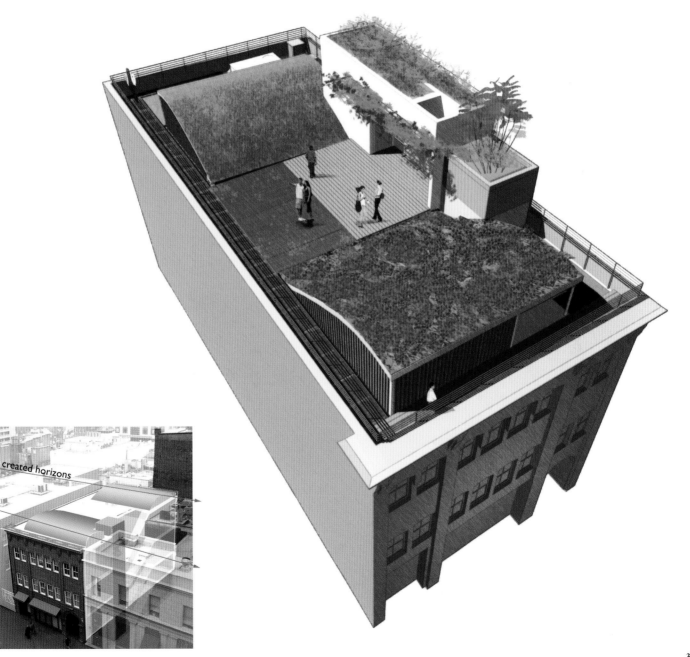

created horizons

40

THE GRATING

The second example of the fusion of the humane and the environmental is the use of an aluminum grating as a walking surface that floats over a thin sedum planting. The standard solution is to separate areas for pedestrians and areas for plants by having pavement next to planting. The floating grate allows plants and humans to coexist at the same location. The grating covers sixty percent of all accessible surfaces on the roof and increases the total green surface of the roof by thirty percent—areas that otherwise would have been lost to paving. Similar to the waves, the multifunctional quality of the grating/vegetation detail gets the most use out of the small roof for humans and for ecology.

Besides its functionality, there is also an educational aspect to the grating. A visitor walking for the first time on the ASLA roof is surprised to find plants above and below her or his feet. The importance of the vegetation as an infrastructural element is thereby highlighted.

The two design elements, the wave and the grating, exemplify how the designers tailored green roof technology to maximize the experiential quality of the roof and sustain a maximum of environmental performance. The task was to go "inside" green roof technology, find its inherent aesthetic potentials, and to design a roof that is not only environmentally sound, but also a destination.

THE PRODUCTION OF WELL BEING

The ASLA roof as a green roof hybrid engages psychological welfare of humans—a topic that was prevalent in the beginning of the last century when roof gardens were propagated for the betterment of the masses, and a topic that should be the next step in green roof development. Thereby the ASLA roof could serve as an example for an expanded notion of sustainability. "Going beyond the environmental necessity" is the future of green roofs, as the German FLL Vice President Klaus Neumann puts it. He claims that the implementation of green roofs will be driven more by public health concerns and international city marketing strategies than by actual environmental performance.[28] In contrast to the socialist cause of the twenties, the argument today is an economic one as outlined by the futurologist Erik Händeler:

> In the future it will be less about the flow of information between people and technology, but about the flow of information between and inside people themselves. In order to open up this potential, a new basic

innovation is needed: psycho-social, holistic health. It will open up the work reserves of the information worker and will form the decisive location factor for the economical success of an information society: motivation, creativity, team work, basically immaterial factors in an increasingly immaterial economy.[29]

The holistic well-being of the workers is not solely a humanitarian cause, it is key to commercial success, and an inspiring built environment is its basis. Neumann believes that agglomerations with an active roof culture will have an economic edge in international city marketing: green culture on the roof could and should develop to an important element of city marketing like the plazas of Barcelona, the fountains of Rome, the world heritage of the landscapes around Potsdam, or the canals of Venice.[30]

IX. A Vision

HOW IT COULD BE

Klaus Neumann's vision is not so far away from reality in some German towns. Realistic distribution of various roof designs and usages after twenty years of green roof policies in a metropolitan region can be observed in Stuttgart. Since the 1980s, the city has had strict ordinances for green roof implementation. The impact of these ordinances is reflected in the Königsstrasse, where roofs are in a diverse state of transition. Some roofs are still bare, unused, and waiting for their transformation. Some older buildings have been retrofitted with green roofs ranging from grass to sedum roofs. Some roofs are used for parking, some house offices, and some are occupied by distinct age groups. In summer, one above-ground shopping mall parking lot is transformed into a highly frequented habitat for twenty-somethings—a beach bar with three inches of white sand, volleyball nets, deck chairs, palm trees, and outdoor divans in the middle of the city. It is probably not one of the most environmentally active roofs, but for sure one of the most beloved. In winter, the roof is disassembled and used for parking until the days get longer again.

HOW IT IS

With the notable exceptions of cities like Chicago or Portland, the United States is still far away from a social green roof culture, though there is growing momentum. In 2005 the U.S. green roof industry experienced a

Offices

Sedum roof

Roof beach

Grass roof

Gray roof

Roof parking

very encouraging growth spurt of a seventy percent increase. An impressive number of about 2,150,000 square feet of green roofs were actually built in the country. [31] However, with about 0.01 percent, the total percentage of green roofs on the whole U.S. roof market is still miniscule. How long will it take for green roofs to make a visible dent in the huge roof market of the United States? [32]

Germany supposedly has the highest implementation rate of green roofs in the world, but it took thirty years of research and twenty years of proactive green roof policies to reach the current market rate of about seven percent. [33] A transfer of this rate to the huge U.S. roof market would be a seven hundredfold increase to the current rate.

If more than seven percent of the yearly U.S. roof demand were to become green in 2037, a sizable sixty-eight square miles would be installed per year—larger than the total area of all green roofs that were built during the last thirty years in Germany. [34] The U.S. green roof industry would mushroom to an annual seven-billion-dollar enterprise.

A lot of things would have to change before green roofs can become a mainstream option. Smart policies need to be invented on all levels, viable vegetation technologies need to be found for all the various climates and vegetation zones of the United States, and the green roof industry has to offer simpler and lower-priced products.

HOW IT SHOULD BE

If one were to give an overly optimistic outlook of the future of roofs, it could be speculated that more U.S. cities will join Chicago and Portland in recognizing the economic value of green infrastructure. Cities will recognize that a healthy and inspiring live and work environment is actually profitable not only for an individual firm but for a whole region. It will be widely acknowledged that roofs possess environmental and experiential qualities that are vital for the well-being of an information society. Their seclusion, views, and exposure to the elements will be valued as a counterbalance to long hours spent in front of the screen. In dense urban environments they will complement the available public outdoor space palette on the ground by providing a private to semi-public space of retreat high above, following the ASLA example. Health experts will underline the benefit of getting up once in a while, walking up some stairs, and exposing one's senses to the amplified forces of sun, wind, and air on a roof (followed by a warning not to stay too long in the sun), thereby effectively clearing one's mind for the tasks ahead. After the initial phase of promoting green roofs to solve environmental and visual problems, accessible green roofs will be valued as a mental health tool—part of the necessary infrastructure of a true sustainable city. Health insurance agencies will offer incentives for employers to improve workplace conditions, gradually liberating workers from their cubicles, requesting quotas for natural lighting, and adding quotas for private outdoor space per capita. In denser urban environments, it will be found that the quota can only be met when unused roof space is transformed into accessible roofs. Those roofs will not only be equipped with little terraces over waterproofing membranes, they will be fully covered with plants in order to pay for the realistically adjusted stormwater fees. Green roof hybrids (light, green, and enjoyable) will increase in popularity and installation costs will decrease substantially.

The American roofscape will change over time. Depending on the program, budget, and context there will be a range of typologies: traditional roof gardens and terraces to green roof hybrids, roofs for environmental remediation, for biodiversity, for food production (plants and animals), for energy production (solar panels), for cleaning grey water, for sport, night life, dining, living (penthouses), religious ceremonies, parking, storage, and last and least, mechanical units.

In the US, **932 sq miles** of rooftops are newly built or resurfaced each year - aproximately **13** times the area of Washington DC.[1]

Currently **0.01%** of these roofs are green = 0.08 sq miles[2]

In Germany, **68 sq miles** of rooftops are newly built or resurfaced each year - aproximately **1** times the area of Washington DC.[3]

Currently **7%** of these roofs are green = **5.2 sq miles**[4]

If the US increased its rate of green roof construction to equal Germany's, it would cover **68 sq miles** per year, aproximately **1** times the area of Washington DC.

1 Research by Freedonia Group
2 Green Roof Industry Survey 2004 & 2005 by Green Roofs for Healthy Cities
3 Deutscher Dachdeckerverband (German Roofbuilder Association)
4 Fritz Hammerle. http://www.haemmerle-gruendach.de

5 miles

Notes

1 Forschungsgesellschaft Landschaftsentwicklung Landschaftsbau e.V., *Guideline for the Planning, Execution and Upkeep of Green-Roof Sites* (Bonn, Germany: FLL, 2002).

2 Nigel Dunnett and Noël Kingsbury, *Planting Green Roofs and Living Walls* (Portland, Oreg.: Timber Press, 2004).

3 Second CIAM in Frankfurt, 1929.

4 Henry Maasz, *Gartentechnik und Gartenkunst* (Nordhausen, Germany: Heinrich Killinger Verlagsgesellschaft, 1930), 518–21.

5 Le Corbusier: "The Conquest of the Flat Roof," *Das Neue Frankfurt: Monatsschrift fuer die Fragen der Grosstadtgestaltung,* (Frankfurt: Englert und Schlosser, 1927), 167–69.

6 Ibid.

7 Andrés Martínez, *Dwelling on the Roof* (Barcelona, Spain: Editorial Gustavo Gili, 2005), 130–36.

8 Gerda Gollwitzer and Werner Wirsing, *Dachflächen: Bewohnt, belebt, bepflanzt* (München, Germany: Georg D.W. Callwey, 1971).

9 HVAC stands for Heating, Ventilation, and Air Condition.

10 Andrés Martínez, *Dwelling on the Roof*, 12–15.

11 Roland Stifter, *Dachgaerten: Gruene Inseln in der Stadt* (Stuttgart, Germany: Ulmer Verlag, 1988), 11–12.

12 Eduard Rüber, *Das Rasendach die wohlfeilste: dauerhafteste und feuersicherste Eindeckungsart* (Hannover: Schäfer, 2002 (republished)).

13 Reinhard Bornkamm, "Vegetation und Vegetationsentwicklung auf Kiesdaechern," *Vegetation* 10 (1961): 1–24.

14 Manfred Köhler and Melissa Keeley, "Berlin, Green Roof Technology and Policy Development," *Green Roofs: Ecological Design and Construction* (Atglen, Pa.: Schiffer Publishing, 2005), 108.

15 Hans-Joachim Liesecke, "Entstehung und Entwicklung der extensiven Dachbegrünung," *Dach+Grün* (Stuttgart) 4 (2005).

16 Hans-Joachim Liesecke, "Vegetationstechnische Gesichtspunkte bei der Begrünung von Flachdächern," *Deutscher Gartenbau* 29 (1975) 1223–26.

17 Original text in German translated by author from: Alexander Mitscherlich, *Die Unwirtlichkeit unserer Staedte: Anstiftung zum Unfrieden* (Frankfurt, Germany: Suhrkamp, 1965).

18 Fritz Hämmerle, *Der Gründachmarkt leidet unter Wachstumshemmern,* (2005), http://www.haemmerle-gruendach.de/marktspiegel.html.

19 Verbal communication with Dr. Stephan Brenneisen.

20 Elias Landolt, "Orchideen-Wiesen in Wollishofen (Zürich): ein erstaunliches Relikt aus dem Anfang des 20. Jahrhunderts," *Zürich: Vierteljahresschrift der Naturforschenden Gesellschaft in Zürich* (2001), 146/2–3, 41–51.

21 Ibid.

22 Stephan Brenneisen, "Green Roofs: Recapturing Urban Space for Wildlife: a Challenge for Urban Planning and Environmental Education," paper submitted for: Greening Rooftops for Sustainable Communities, conference, Washington DC, (2005).

23 Ed Snodgrass, "100 Extensive Green Roofs: Lessons Learned," paper submitted for: Greening Rooftops for Sustainable Communities, conference, Washington DC, (2005).

24 Paul Kephart, "Living Architecture: An Ecological Approach," paper submitted for: Greening Rooftops for Sustainable Communities, conference, Washington DC, (2005).

25 Verbal communication with Heinz Müller of Atelier 5.

26 Le Corbusier, *Une petite maison* (Zürich: Aux Editions d'Architecture, 1954), 39–41.

27 Gerda Gollwitzer and Werner Wirsing, *Dachflächen: Bewohnt, belebt, bepflanzt.*

28 Klaus Neumann, "Grüne Dächer als Herausforderung für die Zukunft," *International Green Roof Congress 14–15 September, 2004 Nürtingen* (Berlin, Germany: International Green Roof Association, 2004).

29 Erik Händeler, *Die Geschichte der Zukunft* (Moers, Germany: Brendow Verlag, 2003), 242.

30 Klaus Neumann, "Grüne Dächer als Herausforderung für die Zukunft."

31 Green Roofs for Healthy Cities, "Final Report Green Roof Industry Survey," www.greenroofs.net, (2006).

32 Market Research by Freedonia Group.

33 Seven percent for the whole German roof market (area number). Since half of Germany's yearly roof demand is sloped roofs and almost all green roofs are currently built on flat roofs, the rate is actually fourteen percent for all newly built or resurfaced flat roofs. See Fritz Hämmerle, *Der Gründachmarkt leidet unter Wachstumshemmern.*

34 There is no exact survey of all existing green roofs in Germany, but an estimated fifty square miles supposedly exist.

Part II:
The ASLA
Green Roof

Finished Construction

(three months after planting)

When the American Society of Landscape Architects (ASLA) was faced with the necessity of resurfacing the roof of its headquarters in Washington, DC, in 2005, they decided to take the opportunity of displaying environmental stewardship by building an exemplary green roof. The ASLA assembled a task force to oversee the project and solicited proposals from several firms for its design. After the selection process, the renowned landscape architecture firm Michael Van Valkenburgh Associates (MVVA) came on board with the bold promise to explore the next generation of green roofs. Choosing an experimental approach, MVVA wanted to explore green roof technology as a medium for landscape architecture and to see where the inherent potentials of the technology would lead the design. In their quest, MVVA was consulted by Conservation Design Forum (CDF), who brought in extensive experience in the construction of green roofs, and by an extensive team of structural engineers, architects, plumbing specialists, horticulturalists, and green roof manufacturers. The roof was designed and built in the very short period of one year and opened officially at the end of April 2006 (keep in mind that the following images show the roof shortly after planting and depict the point of departure; the plants are not fully grown in).

As promised by the designers, the demonstration aspect of the ASLA roof went far beyond the mere testing of suitable plants and materials. During the design process the team found that the roof's accessibility to visitors could be a bigger design driver than previously thought, and the aspect of creating a place for human inhabitation came to the fore. Today the roof is as much an environmental asset as a recreational one. It serves not only as an exemplary project for green infrastructure in the city but also for retrofitting the city to human needs. Achieving this overdue potential on a tiny roof like the ASLA was not easy. The aspect of human inhabitation posed considerable challenges for the designers, and the learning curve achieved here will hopefully benefit the field.

Part III:
Roof Index
A–Z

A–Z contents

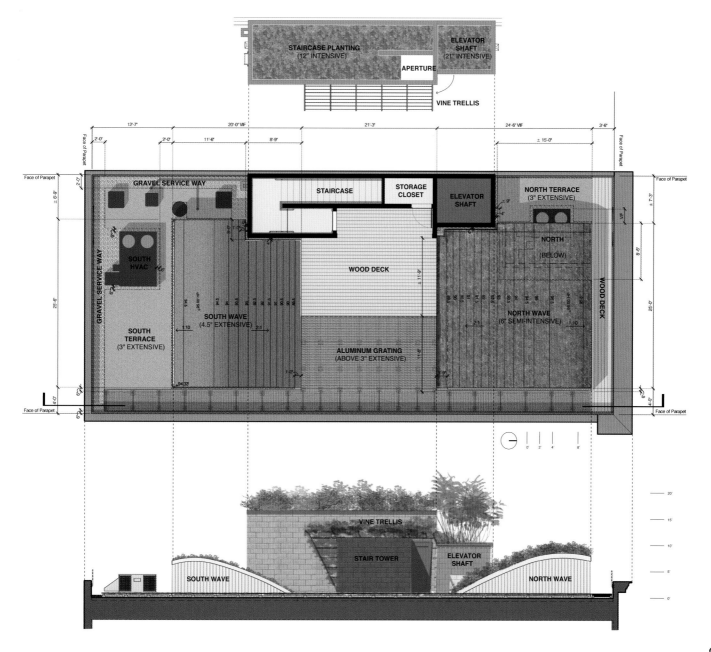

STAIRCASE PLANTING
(12" INTENSIVE)

ELEVATOR
SHAFT
(21" INTENSIVE)

APERTURE

VINE TRELLIS

GRAVEL SERVICE WAY

STAIRCASE

STORAGE
CLOSET

ELEVATOR
SHAFT

NORTH TERRACE
(3" EXTENSIVE)

Face of Parapet

Face of Parapet

SOUTH
HVAC

WOOD DECK

NORTH
(BELOW)

GRAVEL SERVICE WAY

SOUTH
TERRACE
(3" EXTENSIVE)

SOUTH WAVE
(4.5" EXTENSIVE)

NORTH WAVE
(6" SEMI-INTENSIVE)

WOOD DECK

ALUMINUM GRATING
(ABOVE 3" EXTENSIVE)

Face of Parapet

Face of Parapet

VINE TRELLIS

STAIR TOWER

ELEVATOR
SHAFT

SOUTH WAVE

NORTH WAVE

Air handlers

The roof hosts two large air handlers and three smaller air-conditioning units (see also "Existing Roof"). The two large air handlers pump air into the second and third floors, and the three smaller units supply the basement, the lobby, and the first floor. The two big units, which are located in the middle of the roof, posed a major obstacle for the roof design.

In a first design iteration, the design team proposed relocating the two larger units, each with a footprint of eight-by-six feet and weighing around one thousand pounds, on top of the new stair tower. Since the roof of the tower would be erected over the existing structural beams of the building, it would be capable of bearing the additional weight of the air handlers. Vines were proposed to hide the units from sight and the elevated location would have reduced the noise impact

However, technical and financial issues made this solution unfeasible. Ductwork had to be extended from the original locations to the roof of the tower. The longer ducts would have exceeded the performance capacity of the units, and new air handlers would have to have been acquired.

The client rejected this solution—not solely for cost reasons, but also to maintain the feasibility of the ASLA roof as a role model. The client then asked the team to look for alternative locations, which proved not to be an easy task.

The requirements for service and operation of air handlers are quite stringent. The units have to be accessible for maintenance and require a clear space between two and three feet around them. Three feet of overhead clearance has to be maintained

directly over the exhaust openings of the units. The biggest constraint though is that the air handlers can only move a short distance from their original locations in order to maintain their full capacity.

Leaving the units in their original place would have precluded incorporating the planted "waves," which had already been designed and approved by the client. The study revealed that the two air handlers would eradicate the waves. Hiding of the units inside the waves was not possible given access and vertical clearance requirements.

After evaluating several options balancing mechanical, structural, aesthetic, and financial considerations, the two large air handlers came to rest behind the south mound and halfway under the north wave, not far away from their original locations.

Placing the air handler under the north wave produced a sophisticated detail. The north wave bridges over the air handler, stopping short at the ventilators of the unit. A steel column erected right on top of an existing truss supports the wave at its outermost edge.

The waves are undoubtedly the most prominent design elements on the roof. Without the bridge, the air handler would have seriously impacted the north wave as a recognizable form from street level (see "Visibility"). Interestingly enough, the bridge is the only location on the roof where it is revealed that the plants of the north wave grow in only six inches of soil.

The mechanical equipment on the roof was a bigger challenge for the design team than expected. Since the majority of roofs

are dedicated to mechanical units of all sorts, the struggle of the ASLA team should serve as a lesson for similar roof conversions. Early cooperation with HVAC specialists is key to identifying the special requirements and limitations of mechanical equipment.

By and large, the real problem lies in the continued use of an outdated and inefficient heating and ventilation technology that uses roofs as a convenient storage space. One can only speculate how the new ASLA roof design would have profited from a similarly high-profile retrofit of the heating and cooling system of the building.

TOP LEFT: Existing locations of air handlers

BELOW LEFT: Relocation studies of air handlers; from top to bottom: roof design; air handlers' impact on design if they are to remain; air handlers on stair tower; air handlers behind and under waves (final solution, diagram by MVVA)

TOP MIDDLE AND RIGHT: Air handler behind south wave; air handler below north wave (model studies by MVVA)

BELOW RIGHT: Air handler below north wave; exhaust openings had to be left unobstructed.

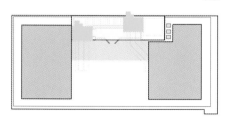

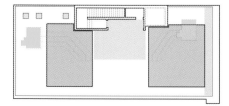

Aperture

TOP: Aperture sketch (by MVVA)
BOTTOM LEFT: 3D study (by MVVA)
BOTTOM RIGHT: Built product

The stair tower leading up to the roof is penetrated by a skylight at its north wall, which floods the space with daylight. The designers stress the importance of glimpsing the flame sumacs behind the stair tower through the aperture (see "Planting"). They also liked the idea of having the play of shadow and light on the otherwise dark north wall, effectively opening up the boxlike appearance of the tower. The wall and the skylight are among the first elements visitors see after arriving at the top of the stairs (see "Stair Tower").

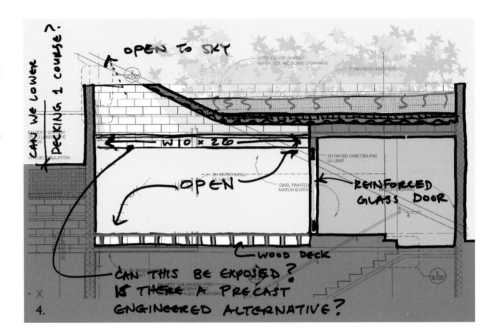

68

Biodiversity

Green roofs can create habitats for flora and fauna even in dense urban locations through the careful composition of growing medium, plants, and the manipulation of microclimatic conditions. The sturdy structure of the existing ASLA roof offered unique opportunities because it allowed the placement of growing medium deeper than six inches in certain areas—more than what extensive green-roof constructions typically tolerate (see "Load Capacity").

The deeper substrates are important for the survival of invertebrates, such as spiders and beetles, that typically freeze to death in thinner growing media. In soils deeper than six inches, they can survive the cold. Furthermore, plants can better withstand dry and hot periods in deeper growing media, when there is some moisture left in the lower regions. After a drought, the deeper growing media act as islands of seed dispersal for shallower areas where plants did not survive. Three out of the six planting zones of the ASLA roof offer growing media of six inches and deeper (see "Planting").

Another factor that distinguishes the ASLA roof from other green roofs is the varying solar exposures of its green surfaces, resulting in different microclimatic conditions. On most green roofs the vegetated surfaces are flat and receive a constant amount of solar radiation (except when shaded by other buildings). The different exposures and soil depths of the north and south waves created varying moisture regimes that will influence the distribution of animals and plants (see "Monitoring").

Flowering chive and thread-leaved tickseed attract butterflies on the ASLA roof.

A · B · C

Building

A · B · C

Modeled after nineteenth-century industrial architecture, the steel-frame structure was a speculative development by Development Resources, Inc., begun in 1995 and designed by Russell Sears and Associates with three above-grade floors and a basement for a total of 12,800 square feet. The ASLA is the original owner and has occupied it since 1997, employing forty-five to fifty persons in the headquarters.

ASLA building with interior vertical circulation visible (photomontage by MVVA)

Construction Costs

The final construction cost for the ASLA roof amounted to approximately $950,000. The ASLA stresses that $600,000 of the budget was used for the architectural components of the roof, mainly to create access (see "Stair Tower"). The remaining $350,000 was spent for the green parts of the roof: the relocation of the air handlers, the two waves, the grating over the sedum, and all other plantings. The ASLA noted that the project budget was not only strained by working on an occupied building with limited accessibility for construction staging and storage, it was also strongly influenced by a surge of material and labor costs caused by the Gulf Coast hurricanes of 2005. These factors left the ASLA with a wide budget gap shortly before commencement of construction.

Faced with this crisis, the organization discussed scaling back the design to a generic green roof, accessible only to maintenance personnel. The reduced version would have probably cost around $150,000 and would have easily fit the budget (according to the estimates of the ASLA, a conventional resurfacing would have cost more than $100,000). In the end, the organization did not choose this option and stayed with the original design by MVVA. It started an intense fundraising effort and solicited contributions from ASLA members, product donations by manufacturers, and construction service discounts from contractors.

If the society had opted for a green roof carpet, the core mission of landscape architecture—to mesh and advance humans, fauna, and flora through thoughtful design—would not have applied to its own headquarters. An inaccessible green roof would have resulted in a minor contribution to the physical and mental health of the building inhabitants—a seriously diminishing mission and the relevance of the whole project. The current product might be higher in cost, but its collective gains are much higher as well.

On the whole, one would have wished that the employment of green roof technology for constructing enjoyable outdoor spaces yielded a low-cost product that could be widely applied. Considering that most of the ASLA budget was spent on creating access to the roof, lightweight accessible green roofs might turn out to be more cost effective for new construction than for existing buildings. Still, the current project is less costly than a traditional roof garden, and those costs will decrease even more once green roof technology has turned into a mainstream application.

A · B · C

Context

A · B · C

Drainage

The general concept for green roofs is not to drain storm water as fast as possible, but rather the opposite. The capability of green roofs to store a certain amount of rain water and to delay the run off of severe storms is what makes them so valuable in urban agglomerations. Nevertheless, sufficient drainage is an important consideration in green roof design, since standing water not only presents a long-term risk for waterproofing and reduces insulation capacity on inverted roofs, but also causes plant roots to suffocate and rot. In general, a delicate balance has to be found between the storage and the drainage of storm water on green roofs.

In case of the ASLA roof, the existing roof drained toward two internal drain inlets on the bottom of two inverted trapezoids. The design team changed the existing drainage pattern in order to facilitate the construction process of the roof. The new roof relocates the two drain inlets to the east parapet and slopes the whole roof as one plane with a gradient of two percent from west to east. Roofs of that gradient are referred to as low-sloped or flat roofs, because two percent is considered to be the minimum slope for positive drainage.

All of the new roof elements sit now in one consistent slope instead of an inverted trapezoid. The change helps direct water away from the stair tower as the new highpoint and substantially eases the construction of the two waves, which would have otherwise landed right on top of the former drain inlets.

In a reversal of the old roof system, the waterproofing is now laid onto the existing flat steel deck, whereas the insulation above it forms the two percent cross slope. According to the consulting manufacturers, not much water will reach the waterproofing since most of it will be captured by drain mats and the growing substrate above (see "Roof Section").

Yet, the area below the two waves required special attention as Chris Counts, MVVA's project manager and lead designer, recalls: "One thing we were concerned about after we decided to slope the roof in one direction was the fact that the waves were directly in the path of the water movement. This concern was addressed by covering the entire area of the roof insulation with a thin drainage layer that can receive compressive loading levels and still move water."

Once the portion of the water that is not absorbed and utilized by the green roof reaches the eastern side of the roof, two internal drains return it to the storm-water system of the city. A flow meter measures the ultimate amount of water released into the grid (see "Monitoring"). The design team proposed to collect the excess roof water in a cistern for supplemental irrigation, but a strict interpretation of the building codes prevented this solution. For the moment, the pipe system is set up to be retrofitted with an overflow to a future storage device, which could be used to irrigate the lower courtyard space, conserving the use of potable water.

73

Drainage

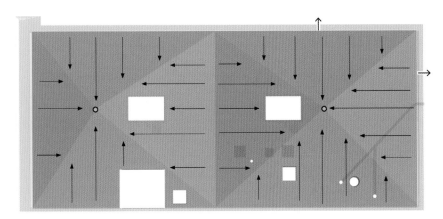

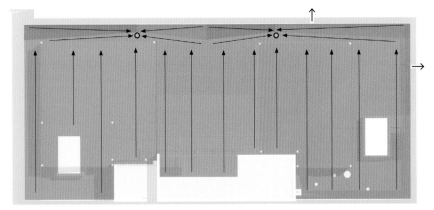

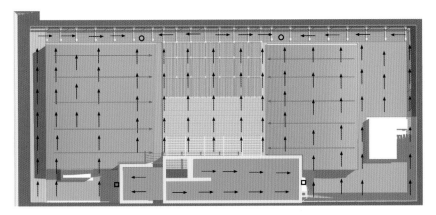

Education

An important factor for the ASLA retrofit was to showcase the contribution landscape architects can make to the current green roof development. An outreach program to local universities, green roof tours, and a maintenance outreach to local schools are underway. The president of the ASLA, Dennis Carmichael, stated:

> This is a landmark investment for our profession, demonstrating the state of the art for green roofs. We want to position landscape architects at the forefront of this emerging practice, and we all have a stake in the success of this project. If we don't take the lead now in designing green roofs, then other design professions will be more than happy to do so.

Carmichael's concerns are well-founded. In Germany only one in seven green roofs is built with the input of landscape architects. The majority are built by landscape contractors and green roof manufacturers.

The low percentage has various reasons. Foremost, green roofs are understood as a technical challenge, and the task is given over to technicians and not designers. Secondly, German green roofs grew into a mass application that, in most cases, did not need the help of a landscape architect. However, European landscape architects have a tradition of making important contributions to the development of green roofs and have decisively shaped the technology through research and built projects in the last thirty years.[1] Now that the technology has finally crossed the Atlantic, American landscape architects can continue this tradition. As U.S. landscape architects play catch-up, they will have to adjust the technology to the varied climate and vegetation conditions of the U.S. and they have to help make the still overpriced technology economically feasible for the U.S. market.

This is a landmark investment for our profession, demonstrating the state of the art for green roofs. We want to position landscape architects at the forefront of this emerging practice, and we all have a stake in the success of this project.

—Dennis Carmichael, President, ASLA

Erosion

Obviously, roof surfaces are particularly exposed to weather conditions, especially sun, wind, and rain. On the ASLA roof, the granular substrate of the two waves, with gradients up to thirty-three percent, is in danger of being washed down by heavy downpours.

As a counter measurement, the designers of the ASLA roof chose a two fold approach. They used a degradable erosion blanket and a permanent slope stabilization net in the slopes of the two waves.

The erosion blanket is laid over the growing medium of the two waves and prevents surface erosion. The blanket is a degradable thin straw mat with natural fiber reinforcing. The danger of erosion is higher right after installation, before plants can fully cover the surface. Once the blanket is degraded (after one or two growing seasons), the plants will cover more of the growing medium.

However, even fully grown plants will not be able to sufficiently stabilize the slopes. Many of the selected plants are adapted to erosion and do not have extensive root systems to hold soil in place. Secondly, the planting selection is experimental (see "Planting"); the substrate needs to be stabilized in the case of eventual plant failure. Therefore the team added a slope-stabilization net—a cellular confinement system made of polyethylene and anchored by steel cables. The net is as deep as the planting area and the growing medium is retained in small diamond-shaped pockets (about six inches by six inches). The polyethylene sheets themselves are perforated to allow water to drain downhill.

Existing Roof

LEFT: Cut through the built-up former roof: PVC membrane, insulation, steel decking, and supporting structure; insulation and membrane were removed later for the new construction

RIGHT: Photo collage of former ASLA roof (by MVVA)

The former ASLA roof consisted of a steel metal deck overlaid with an insulation layer covered by a PVC waterproofing membrane as the top layer. There are two access hatches on the roof that can be reached by climbing up a ladder. Various mechanical units are distributed on the roof (see "Air Handlers").

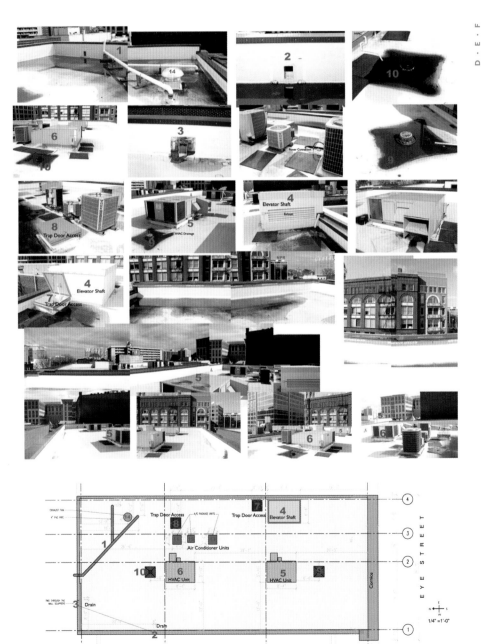

Grating

The grating/vegetation system covers sixty percent of all accessible surfaces and symbolizes the fusion of the environmental and social agenda of the roof (see Part I, p. 41).

The basis of the grating consists of a grid of concrete footers supporting a structural steel frame that holds the aluminum panels. On a roof every unnecessary perforation is avoided, in order to decrease the risk of leakage. Therefore, the concrete footers are not connected to the roof structure, but sit directly on the insulation boards below.

The aluminum grating is a deviation from the galvanized steel finishes of other metal elements on the roof (handrails, stair-tower trellis, waves) and was chosen because of its light weight and low conductivity. The individual grate panels need to be lifted up by maintenance personnel—mainly for weeding during the establishment phase of the sedum carpet below (see "Maintenance").

Extensive studies were undertaken to allow sufficient sunlight for plant growth below (see "Planting"), resulting in opening widths of one inch. The team decided to compromise accessibility (the grating is unsuitable for high heels) in favor of plant growth. As it turned out, the lightly shaded planting areas below the grate are the most vigorous growing areas on the roof.

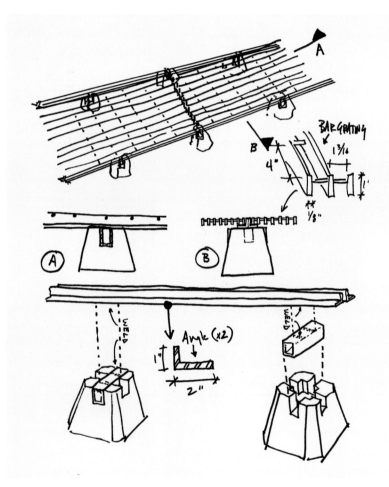

Roof plan speculating the expected
foot traffic (dashed lines), resulting
in a specific plant distribution
between aluminum grates (study
by MVVA)

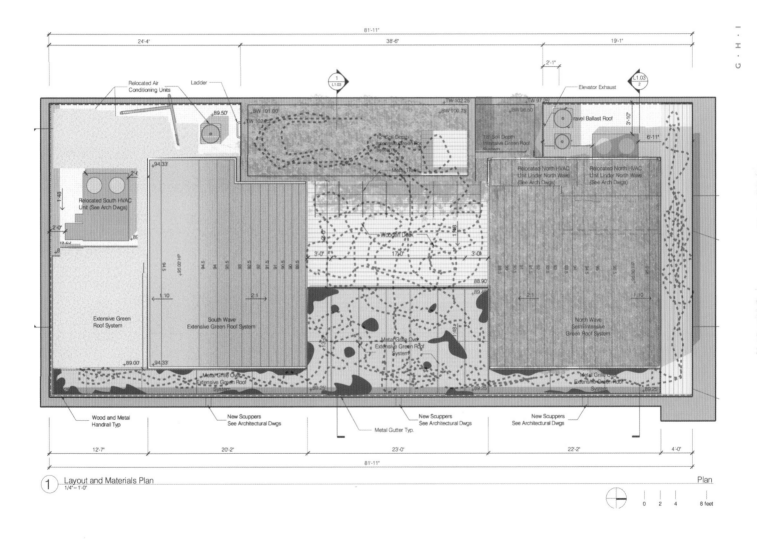

Grating

Construction sequence:
1: Installation of root barrier over waterproofing membrane
2: Placement of insulation boards and thin aeration and rain mat on root barrier
3: Installation of thicker water-retention and drain mat

4: Distribution of growing medium on filter fabric
5: Installation of concrete grating footings and aluminum support beams
6–7: Successive planting of plugs and fastening of grates
8: Final product

G · H · I

Insulation

Foam is not usually associated with the construction of landscapes. However, for on-structure landscapes the use of foam is very common, since the light weight of the material is perfectly suited for filling and building up grade in conditions where weight counts. High compressive-strength values can be achieved with foam and the material is even used as fill below highway onramps (Geofoam).

The ASLA roof employs a common type of foam, extruded polystyrene, to achieve its insulation and to construct the topography of the roof. Pure solid polystyrene is a petroleum product; it is a colorless, hard plastic with limited flexibility. The solid plastic can be expanded into a foam through the use of heat. Extruded polystyrene boards are suitable for outdoor use because they consist of a closed-cell foam with high compressive strength, which resists moisture and retains insulation values even in wet conditions (but only for a limited period of time).

Chris Counts, the project manager from MVVA, stresses the importance of the material for the design of the roof: "Foam creates the artificial topography that the entire design sits on. It directs water to the drains, provides insulation for the building, and it makes the signature design element of the roof—the waves—possible. This material is the spatial engine of the design."

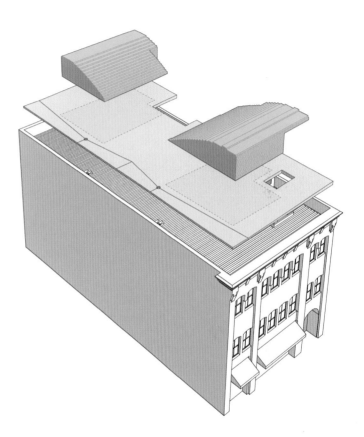

Load Capacity

The load capacity of an existing roof structure is the most decisive number (besides the budget) guiding the design of a green roof. In every project where a green roof is added to an existing roof structure, the structural engineer first determines the total load capacity of the existing structure by studying the available construction documents and the roof itself. The total load capacity of a roof must be greater than the sum of its dead and live loads. The dead load is the weight of the structure itself and any permanent materials that are always present at the same place on the structure. The live load defines the weight limits of temporary elements on the roof like snow, people, temporary and movable objects, or window-washing equipment.

Once the dead load of the existing roof is calculated, the structural engineer determines what the live load requirements are, based on the building code minimum roof or snow load, or on the occupancy classification the architect and client desire. The dead load and live load are then subtracted from the total load capacity in order to determine the additional load that can be applied. The green roof load typically includes the waterproofing, root barrier, insulation, water retention and drainage layer, filter fabric, growing medium (in full saturation), and plants. The rest of the design process of a green roof is then characterized by a back and forth between the structural engineer and the landscape architect in order to make sure that the proposed green roof design stays within the total load capacity of the roof.

In the case of the ASLA roof, the structural engineer was hired before the design team to evaluate the total load capacity of the roof and to determine the feasibility of a green roof addition without any major structural reinforcement of the roof. The engineers retrieved the original construction documents of the building and inspected the structure on site. They found that the roof was built differently from how it appeared in the drawings. The roof joists between the primary steel beams were not spaced at four feet as indicated but at two and a half feet. The tighter spacing resulted in a total load capacity of 80 pounds per square foot (psf) in the southern third of the roof to 105psf for all other areas, much more than the actual dead and live loads of the roof required and more than roofs of this type and era typically yield. Once the minimum required live load of 30psf (snow) was subtracted, the designers could count on an additional dead load of 50 to 75psf for the green roof system that would be placed on top of the roof structure. Given that extensive green roof systems weigh between 10 to 30psf, the surplus load capacity was a welcome surprise. It led the ASLA to the decision that any future design had to manage without structural reinforcement.

At last, the final weight of the design only utilizes the total load capacity of the roof in the southern third bay, the weakest structural area of the roof; in all other areas the design stays well below the load limit (10 psf under). The areas above the green roof pavilion and the elevator shaft allow the biggest loads since they extend directly above either the existing load-bearing CMU stair shaft or existing steel beams. The design of the waves—the south wave has a thinner four-inch soil section compared to the north wave's six-inch one—is an example of the design's adaptation to the different weight limitations of the roof in those areas.

Thanks to the smart interpretation of the code by the structural engineer, the area of the metal grating could be accepted as a "promenade" or small gathering space. Previously the mandatory account of 30psf for snow load plus the 60 psf for live load needed for small gatherings would have exceeded the total load capacity of the roof in this area. However, the structural engineer remarked that the likelihood of an ASLA party in four feet of snow may be highly improbable and dropped the requirement of adding up the two numbers.

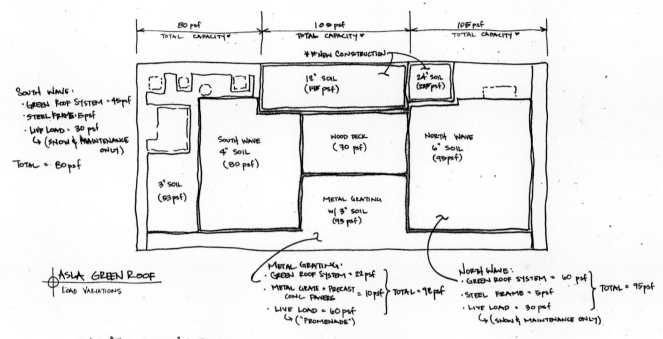

80 psf
TOTAL CAPACITY *

105 psf
TOTAL CAPACITY *

105 psf
TOTAL CAPACITY *

**NEW CONSTRUCTION

12" SOIL
(145 psf)

24" SOIL
(235 psf)

SOUTH WAVE:
· GREEN ROOF SYSTEM = 45 psf
· STEEL FRAME = 5 psf
· LIVE LOAD = 30 psf
  ↳ (SNOW & MAINTENANCE ONLY)

TOTAL = 80 psf

SOUTH WAVE
4" SOIL
(80 psf)

WOOD DECK
(70 psf)

NORTH WAVE
6" SOIL
(95 psf)

3" SOIL
(53 psf)

METAL GRATING
W/ 3" SOIL
(93 psf)

⊕ ASLA GREEN ROOF
LOAD VARIATIONS

METAL GRATING:
· GREEN ROOF SYSTEM = 22 psf
· METAL GRATE + PRECAST   = 10 psf } TOTAL = 92 psf
  CONC. PAVERS
· LIVE LOAD = 60 psf
  ↳ ("PROMENADE")

NORTH WAVE:
· GREEN ROOF SYSTEM = 60 psf
· STEEL FRAME = 5 psf   } TOTAL = 95 psf
· LIVE LOAD = 30 psf
  ↳ (SNOW & MAINTENANCE ONLY)

* NOTE: "TOTAL CAPACITY" IS THE AMOUNT OF ADDITIONAL DEAD LOAD + REQUIRED
LIVE LOAD. DEAD LOAD OF THE EXISTING ROOF STRUCTURE HAS ALREADY BEEN
TAKEN INTO ACCOUNT.
** ORIGINAL ROOF STRUCTURE REMOVED FOR CONSTRUCTION OF STAIR TOWER. NEW ROOF @ THIS LOCATION
ALLOWED FOR DESIGN OF GREEN ROOF SYSTEM WITH HIGHER LOADS. ALL NEW GREEN ROOF LOADS
TRANSMITTED THROUGH LOAD BEARING CMU STAIR TOWER WALLS DIRECTLY TO BUILDING FOUNDATION.

Maintenance

Typically there are two maintenance phases for green roof plantings. Right after planting, the establishment phase begins, lasting up to a couple of years. The goal of this phase is to allow plants to settle in and grow in order to achieve a solid and stable ground cover. After establishment, the long-term maintenance begins, securing the continued survival of the planting area.

In its first growing season, 2006, the maintenance for the establishment of the ASLA roof planting was fairly standard and consisted mainly of watering, replanting, and weeding. Although the majority of the rooftop relied on hand-watering or rainfall, drip irrigation was deemed necessary for the intensive planting areas over the stair tower and the elevator shaft. These two areas are not usually occupied and thus have no guardrails securing against falls. In order to safely access the plants, maintenance personnel have to be connected via ropes to the structure, a practice that is not uncommon, but fairly cumbersome and would have posed an impediment to providing adequate maintenance in these two areas without the irrigation.

On the main roof, the extensive planting areas were irrigated with two oscillating sprinklers placed temporarily in the middle of the waves. Although the extensive planting areas of a green roof have to be able to survive without supplemental irrigation, the young plants needed regular watering to get established in the long and dry Washington, DC, summers. In the extremely dry summer of 2006, during which the temperature on the roof reached as high as 136 degrees, the watering was not frequent enough and

did not reach all areas, leading to plant stagnation and loss. Replanting was necessary in the hottest areas with the thinnest soil profiles, including the southern part of the terrace and the south wave. Later a timer was added to the sprinklers to establish more frequent and shorter periods of watering (see "Planting").

In the areas with more favorable growing conditions, including the deeper and open soils of the stair tower and the milder microclimate below the grates of the terrace, the arrival of unwanted pioneer plants made weeding a necessity. Siberian elm seedlings, spurge, and jewelweed competed with sedum below the grates. For daily weeding a hand tool was used to reach weeds between the one-inch openings in the grates. For larger weeding cycles the aluminum grates of the terrace had to be removed and put back into place.

At the stair tower, five-foot lamb's-quarters, large spurs, and tall grasses were arresting the development of smaller plants like the New Jersey Tea and had to be removed. To reduce future maintenance burdens in this location, a fast-growing groundcover will be added to the plant mix.

At some point a continuous plant cover on the whole roof will be achieved through continued monitoring and selective action based on a better understanding of the particular microclimates and dominant species. At this point the ASLA will be in a position to transition from the current fairly intensive establishment maintenance to an extensive long-term maintenance regime. What will this look like?

The new ASLA roof is the experimental hybrid of an extensive green roof and an intensive roof garden, each of which traditionally comes with a different set of rules regarding tolerable levels of upkeep and appearance. Intensive roof gardens are built for enjoyment and conform to a specific set of aesthetic expectations that change over time but commonly require fairly high levels of maintenance. This active management of die-off and change requires a regime of removal, replanting, and watering. By contrast, extensive green roofs as bioengineering surfaces reside outside of the classic garden tradition. Here, the goal is to limit maintenance to that which is necessary to deliver a clearly defined environmental service. This approach tolerates succession and change as long as the specified function is maintained.

Being a hybrid, the maintenance regime for the ASLA roof lies somewhere in the middle. The traditional garden aesthetic has to be stretched to embrace the unkempt and rough, and the minimal maintenance regime of an extensive landscape has to be adjusted to the user expectations of a small occupied roof in a dense city. If the ASLA roof wants to be a credible model for other semi-extensive recreational green roofs, change and succession have to be accepted as part of the experiment. At the same time, a limited amount of long-term maintenance must be anticipated, including minimal annual weeding, emergency watering during severe droughts, and replanting in instances where no other plants are able to fill in the gap.

Elevator Shaft
Stair Tower · Northern Terrace
←Z→
Southern Terrace
South Wave · Terrace with Grates · North Wave

TOP: Replanting bare patches on the waves
BOTTOM: Tool for weeding the area below grates

The debate about the boundaries of maintenance is currently evolving between the client and MVVA. Thanks to an extensive monitoring program, the understanding that informs these discussions is fairly rich and the experimental disposition of the ASLA roof has already triggered a learning process that allows an ongoing readjustment of maintenance strategies based on plant performance (see "Monitoring").

Mock-up and Models

First experimental model showing various test pieces without any particular order (1/4" = 1', by MVVA)

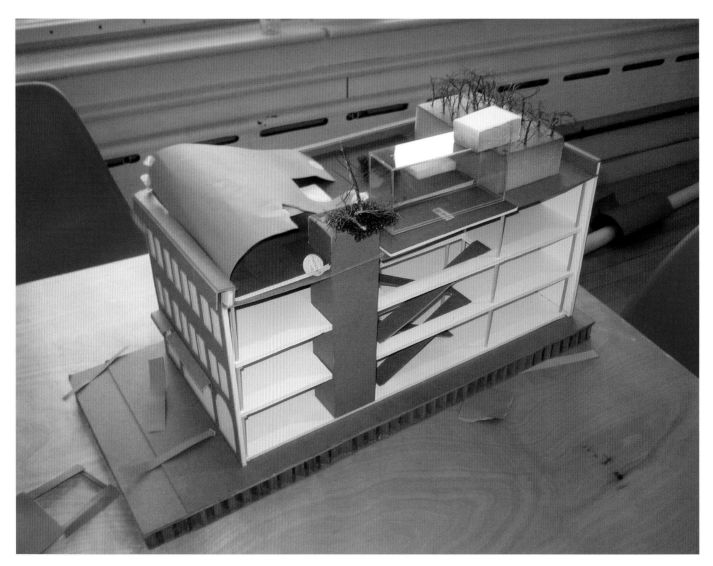

TOP LEFT: Study model with first design iteration (1/4" = 1', by MVVA) **TOP RIGHT:** Final presentation model (1/2" = 1', by MVVA) **BOTTOM LEFT:** 1:1 horizontal layout of ASLA roof in Union Square, New York **BOTTOM RIGHT:** 1:1 vertical layout of north wave

Monitoring

M · O · N

After the roof construction was completed in May 2006, the ASLA requested that MVVA implement a monitoring program to record the performance of the roof in terms of temperature fluctuation, light levels, and storm-water retention. Digital light and temperature meters were positioned close to the surface below the grated areas and the southern and the northern terrace. A mobile reader that in turn can be connected to a computer retrieves the data stored in the meters via infrared communication. The meters were set to record light levels and temperatures every half hour through a period of several months. Richard Hindle of MVVA, who monitors the roof, found: "The south terrace is consistently hotter, with an average temperature of eighty-eight degrees Fahrenheit, which is four degrees hotter than the other horizontal terraces. The maximum temperature was six to nine degrees higher, and the actual fluctuation in temperature was greater on any given day."

Light levels, measured in lumen per square foot, were also continuously higher on the southern terrace—a fact due to the southern exposure and also probably amplified by sunlight reflecting from the gleaming steel of the wave enclosure.

The readings helped explain not only why plant establishment was difficult in the targeted areas (see "Planting"), but also the reasons for the very successful growing environment in the cooler zone beneath the grates.

Besides temperature and light, two electronic flow meters were installed to measure the amount of rainwater finding its way to the two drain inlets on the east side of the roof. The data, transferred directly to a stationary computer, showed retention of about seventy percent of all the rainwater hitting the roof over a six-month period. This means in absolute terms that around 17,800 of 25,500 gallons of water were absorbed by the roof over the course of sixteen rain events with a combined rainfall of 13.5 inches.

In a couple of years the ASLA monitoring will yield the average annual retention capacity of the roof, but the preliminary numbers already show that the ASLA roof retention rates are consistent with the expected performance of comparable green roofs in similar climates.[2] The first data deliver the factual proof that a mass application of green roofs in Washington DC, will deliver a powerful contribution to the ongoing storm-water problems of the city. According to a calculation by the Casey Trees Endowment Fund, about fifteen percent of all combined sewer overflow events in the city could be prevented by greening eighty percent of all future and twenty percent of all existing rooftops in Washington DC.[3]

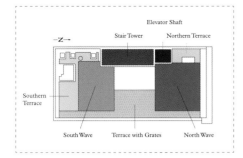

— North Terrace
— Below Grates
— South Terrace

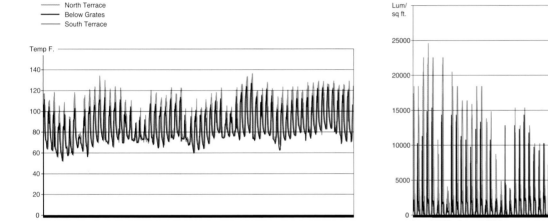

June 7, 2006 – August 7, 2006

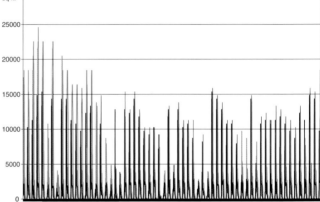

June 7, 2006 – August 7, 2006

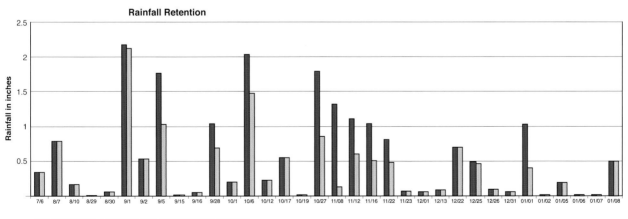

Rainfall Retention

Rain Events from July '06 through January '07 (Month/Day)

■ Total Rainfall: 19.4 inches
□ Rainfall Retained by ASLA Roof: 13.5 inches (70%)

Motives

MONO

As it became clear that the waterproofing membrane of the ASLA headquarters roof needed to be replaced, the society decided that the retrofit should serve as a "demonstration project—both in terms of environmental benefits and aesthetics/amenity value for green roofs and showcase what landscape architects bring to this type of project," according to Nancy Somerville, Executive Vice President of the ASLA. In the beginning, the foremost reason for the retrofit was to green the roof, the provision of better access was secondary and mostly seen by the ASLA as a means of bringing interested visitors to the roof.

Planting

The roof is divided into six distinct planting zones resulting from the different load capacities of the roof (see "Load Capacity"). The depths of the growing medium closely adhere to the structural limits of the roof, with depths of three, four, six, twelve, and twenty-four inches.

Although structural limitations had the strongest impact on the planting, Michael Van Valkenburgh stresses the importance of education and research: "It was understood from the beginning that the roof would be an opportunity to exhibit the variety of green roof planting typologies, and we worked closely with the ASLA and CDF to decide what and where those would be."

All the plants for the roof were planted as plugs or larger. Aside from the intensive green roof areas over the stair tower and elevator shaft, the planting areas are only temporarily irrigated until fully established (see "Maintenance"). After the first growing season, most of the plants are well on their way to establishing themselves.

Planting

Planting plan with original plant list; some species were substituted during and after construction (construction documents by MVVA).

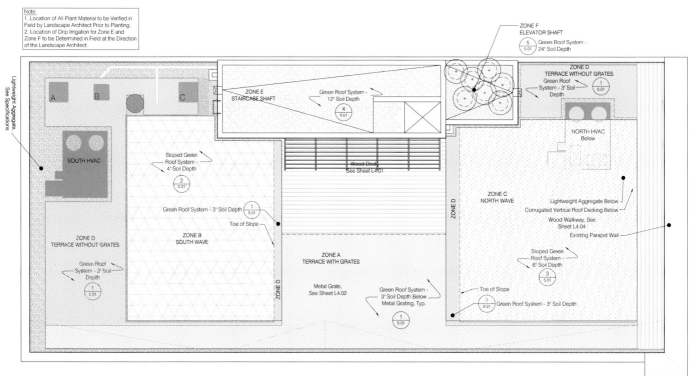

Note:
1. Location of All Plant Material to be Verified in Field by Landscape Architect Prior to Planting.
2. Location of Drip Irrigation for Zone E and Zone F to be Determined in Field at the Direction of the Landscape Architect.

P · Q · R

Lightweight Aggregate, See Specifications

ZONE F
ELEVATOR SHAFT
5/5.01 Green Roof System - 24" Soil Depth

ZONE D
TERRACE WITHOUT GRATES
Green Roof System - 3" Soil Depth
1/5.01

ZONE E
STAIRCASE SHAFT

Green Roof System - 12" Soil Depth
4/5.01

NORTH HVAC
Below

SOUTH HVAC

Sloped Green Roof System - 4" Soil Depth
2/5.01

Green Roof System - 3" Soil Depth
1/5.01

Toe of Slope

ZONE B
SOUTH WAVE

ZONE D
TERRACE WITHOUT GRATES

Green Roof System - 3" Soil Depth
1/5.01

ZONE D

ZONE C
NORTH WAVE

Lightweight Aggregate Below
Corrugated Vertical Roof Decking Below
Wood Walkway, See Sheet L4.04
Existing Parapet Wall

Sloped Green Roof System - 6" Soil Depth
3/5.01

Toe of Slope

Green Roof System - 3" Soil Depth
1/5.01

Wood Deck
See Sheet L401

ZONE A
TERRACE WITH GRATES

Metal Grate, See Sheet L4.02

Green Roof System - 3" Soil Depth Below Metal Grating, Typ.
1/5.01

Planting Schedule

ZONE A - TERRACE WITH GRATES

Succulents

ID.	Qty.	Botanical Name	Common Name	Size	Spacing	Notes
DN	180	Delosperma nubigenum	Ice Plant	2" plug	8" o.c.	
SK	180	Sedum kamtschaticum	Kamtschat Sedum	2" plug	8" o.c.	
SR	180	Sedum reflexum	Spruced-Leaved Stonecrop	2" plug	8" o.c.	
SS	180	Sedum sexangulare	Watch Chain Sedum	2" plug	8" o.c.	
SPF	180	Sedum spurium 'Fuldagut'	Two-Row Stonecrop	2" plug	8" o.c.	
SPJ	180	Sedum spurium 'John Creech'	Two-Row Stonecrop	2" plug	8" o.c.	
SPW	180	Sedum spurium 'White Form'	Two-Row Stonecrop	2" plug	8" o.c.	

ZONE B - SOUTH WAVE

Succulents

ID.	Qty.	Botanical Name	Common Name	Size	Spacing	Notes
SL	172	Sedum lanceolatum	Lance-leaved Stone rop	2" plug	8" o.c.	
SST	172	Sedum stenopetalum	Worm-leaved Stonecrop	2" plug	8" o.c.	
ST	172	Sedum telephioides	Allegheny Stonecrop	2" plug	8" o.c.	

Perennials

ID.	Qty.	Botanical Name	Common Name	Size	Spacing	Notes
CM	172	Chrysopsis mariana	Maryland Aster	2" plug	8" o.c.	
OH	110	Optuntia humifusa	Prickly Pear Cactus	live ears	8" o.c.	
PS	172	Phlox subulata	Moss Phlox	2" plug	8" o.c.	
SV	172	Saxifraga virginiensis	Early Pink	2" plug	8" o.c.	
SC	198	Silene caroliniana	Wild Pink	2" plug	8" o.c.	

ZONE C - NORTH WAVE

Succulents

ID.	Qty.	Botanical Name	Common Name	Size	Spacing	Notes
DN	95	Delosperma nubigenum 'Basutoland'	Ice Plant	2" plug	8" o.c.	
SA	95	Sedum album 'Murale'	White Stonecrop	2" plug	8" o.c.	
SF	95	Sedum floriferum var.	Weihenstephan Gold	2" plug	8" o.c.	
SR	95	Sedum reflexum	Spruced-Leaved Stonecrop	2" plug	8" o.c.	
TC	95	Talium calycinum	Fame Flower	2" plug	8" o.c.	

Grasses

ID.	Qty.	Botanical Name	Common Name	Size	Spacing	Notes
FR	95	Bouteloua gracilis	Blue Grama Grass	2" plug	8" o.c.	
SH	95	Sporobolus heterolepsis	Prairie Dropseed	2" plug	8" o.c.	
EV	95	Elymus virginicus	Virginia Wild Rye	2" plug	8" o.c.	
ES	95	Eragrostis spectabilis	Purple Lovegrass	2" plug	8" o.c.	

Perennials

ID.	Qty.	Botanical Name	Common Name	Size	Spacing	Notes
AF	50	Artemisia frigida	Prairie Sagewort	2 qt	12" o.c.	
TB	50	Tradescantia bracteata	Spiderwort	2 qt	12" o.c.	
GS	50	Gutierrezia sarothrae	Broom Snakeweed	2 qt	12" o.c.	
RH	50	Rudbeckia hirta	Black-eyed Susan	2 qt	12" o.c.	
AT	50	Asclepias tuberosa	Butterfly Milkweed	2 qt	12" o.c.	
AM	50	Achillea millefolium	Yarrow	2 qt	12" o.c.	
SN	50	Solidago nemoralis	Old Field Goldenrod	2 qt	12" o.c.	
AO	50	Allium ostrowskianum	Pink Lily Leek	2 qt	12" o.c.	

ZONE D - TERRACE WITHOUT GRATES

Succulents

ID.	Qty.	Botanical Name	Common Name	Size	Spacing	Notes
DN	125	Delosperma nubigenum	Ice Plant	2" plug	8" o.c.	
SK	110	Sedum kamtschaticum	Kamtschat Sedum	2" plug	8" o.c.	
SR	110	Sedum reflexum	Spruced-Leaved Stonecrop	2" plug	8" o.c.	
SS	110	Sedum sexangulare	Watch Chain Sedum	2" plug	8" o.c.	
SPF	110	Sedum spurium 'Fuldagut'	Two-Row Stonecrop	2" plug	8" o.c.	
SPJ	110	Sedum spurium 'John Creech'	Two-Row Stonecrop	2" plug	8" o.c.	
SPW	110	Sedum spurium 'White Form'	Two-Row Stonecrop	2" plug	8" o.c.	
TC	110	Talium calycinum	Fame Flower	2" plug	8" o.c.	

ZONE E - STAIRCASE SHAFT

ID.	Qty.	Botanical Name	Common Name	Size	Spacing	Notes
CA	20	Ceonanthus americanus	New Jersey Tea	24'-36' ht	24" o.c.	
CP	20	Comptonia peregrine	Sweet Fern	24'-36' ht	24" o.c.	
RA	20	Rhus aromatica	Fragrant Sumac	24'-36' ht	24" o.c.	
RS	16	Rosa carolina	Pasture Rose	18'-24' ht	24" o.c.	

ZONE F - ELEVATOR SHAFT

ID.	Qty.	Botanical Name	Common Name	Size	Spacing	Notes
RC	14	Rhus copalina	Flame Sumac	6'-7' ht.		
CR	3	Campsis radicans 'Madame Galans'	Trumpet Vine	7 gallon		10'-12' ht.

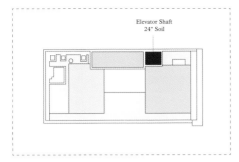

Elevator Shaft
24" Soil

TOP: Elevator shaft planting section (construction documents by MVVA)
BELOW: Plant images by MVVA staff, plant descriptions by Richard Hindle (MVVA) and Marcus de la fleur (CDF)

Elevator Shaft

The area above the elevator shaft is the deepest planting area on the roof with a twenty-four-inch-deep growing medium. It offers the opportunity to plant taller plants and a trumpet vine that will eventually grow over the metal trellis mounted on the stair tower.

The concept of larger vegetation over the structurally strong staircase and elevator shaft appeared in the very early design stages of the project. Since the new stair tower is an extension of the structural system of the building, it could have even supported the weight of large trees. However, the design team recognized that larger trees would be prone to falling during winds due to their exposed location and the limited horizontal dimensions of the planter, which does not allow for an adequate root structure. Thus, a tall shrub was chosen instead. The fourteen flame sumacs will eventually form a dense grove that might in a couple of years be visible from the street. The sumac will be a brilliant red-orange color in fall, visible through the skylight of the staircase shaft (see "Aperture").

Five months after planting, the sumacs are thriving. Given that they can reach up to twenty or thirty feet on the ground, it will be interesting to observe what heights the plants will reach in the limited growing conditions of the planter.

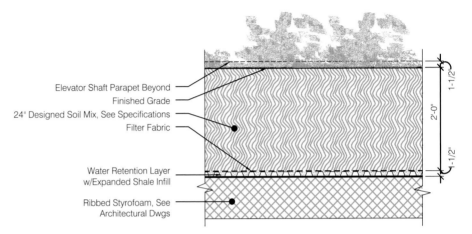

Elevator Shaft Parapet Beyond
Finished Grade
24" Designed Soil Mix, See Specifications
Filter Fabric

Water Retention Layer w/Expanded Shale Infill

Ribbed Styrofoam, See Architectural Dwgs

1-1/2"
2'-0"
1-1/2"

P · Q · R

Campsis radicans "Madame Galans"
Trumpet vine
Vigorous dense creeping foliage and ornate floral displays; provides shade and wildlife interest to the staircase shaft trellis.

Rhus copallina
Flame sumac
Tall slender stems display tufts of foliage and flower panicles high above the roof terraces, insuring visibility at street level. Flame sumac pioneers and colonizes poor soils and provides flame-red fall color.

Planting

TOP: Placement of growing medium onto stair tower
BOTTOM LEFT: Planting of stair tower
BOTTOM RIGHT: Plant development after three months

Stair Tower

The area over the stair tower with twelve-inch-deep growing medium is also intensively planted, albeit with lower-growing shrubs (up to four feet). The fragrant sumac and the pasture rose established themselves very well in the first growing season, whereas the less vigorous New Jersey tea and sweet fern suffered from a substantial weed infestation and will require more time and maintenance before they can cover the whole area (see "Maintenance").

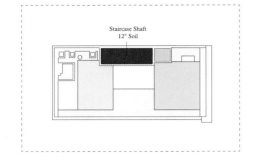
TOP: Stair tower planting section (construction documents by MVVA) **BELOW:** Stair tower shrubs; plant descriptions by Richard Hindle (MVVA) and Marcus de la fleur (CDF)

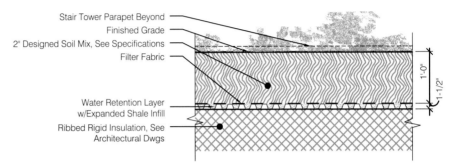

Stair Tower Parapet Beyond
Finished Grade
2" Designed Soil Mix, See Specifications
Filter Fabric

Water Retention Layer w/Expanded Shale Infill
Ribbed Rigid Insulation, See Architectural Dwgs

1'-0"
1 - 1/2"

P · Q · R

Ceonanthus americanus
New Jersey tea
The snowball-like floral display is conspicuous in native meadows and garden beds, bringing aesthetic interest to the staircase shaft plant community. The trial planting at the ASLA will test its viability as a green roof plant.

Comptonia peregrine
Sweet fern
This East Coast native can be found growing in sandy soils and dry hillsides with low organic content, similar to the growing substrate installed on the staircase shaft.

Rhus aromatica
Fragrant sumac
Large colonies offer brilliant scarlet fall color in their native environment along limestone cliffs and rocky bluffs of the Chesapeake Watershed, making it well-suited to exposed conditions.

Rosa carolina
Pasture rose
A rugged rose well suited to meadows, roadsides, and wilder gardens; the thick foliage creates a green cap over the staircase shaft, becoming a conspicuous element in the neighborhood rooftop topography.

South Wave

P · Q · R

The steep slopes of the two waves create varying moisture conditions that result in diverse growing conditions (dry on crest, moist on toe) and different sun exposures. The thinner south wave, with a four-inch-deep substrate, is the test field for perennials native to the region, low growing succulents of the American West, and one native sedum from Pennsylvania (*Sedum telephioides*).

Those plants were chosen because they naturally occur on rocky outcrops or talus slopes, settings comparable to roof tops.

Given that the multitude of climates in the United States differs considerably from those found in temperate northern Europe, the testing of suitable native plant material is probably the single most important research field for the green roof movement in the United States. The plant specialist Ed Snodgrass of Emery Knoll Farms, who delivered most of the plants for the ASLA project, laments that "the American green roof market is still in its infancy. True regional plant lists and reliable natives still elude us."[4] Across the country, research institutions and firms now undertake the testing of indigenous plants with only mixed success.[5]

Whereas the prickly pear cactus on the crest of the south wave (driest point) and the planted perennials (*Phlox subulata, Silene caroliniana*) could establish themselves very well, most of the native sedums planted are in severe distress (*Sedum telephioides*) or have vanished altogether (*Sedum lanceolatum*) due to an extremely dry and hot summer, uneven watering, and birds digging up plants in search of insects. *Sedum stenopetalum* vanished from the south wave after planting and re-emerged after the summer.

Radiation and temperature measurements showed that the south wave is one of the hottest planting areas on the roof (see "Monitoring"). The conditions were so harsh that not even weeds would colonize this area as they did in other open surfaces on the roof. The situation worsened because of the absence of four hundred perennials that had been ordered but were not available at the time of planting. These additional plants would have shaded the bare surfaces of the wave, blocking the substrate from collecting the heat energy and increased moisture in the air.

The failing native sedums were finally replaced with more drought-tolerant succulents, mostly of European origin (*Sedum album, Sedum reflexum, Sedum spurium, Sedum cauticola, Sedum sexangulare, Sempervivum tectorum, Orostachys boehmeri, Sedum floriferum*). Instead of using plugs grown in peat moss, Richard Hindle of MVVA, who monitors the roof, chose larger, mature plants that were grown in green roof substrate, thereby reducing the shock of transplanting. The designers plan to add more plants in the next growing season in order to increase diversity and better protect against future plant failures.

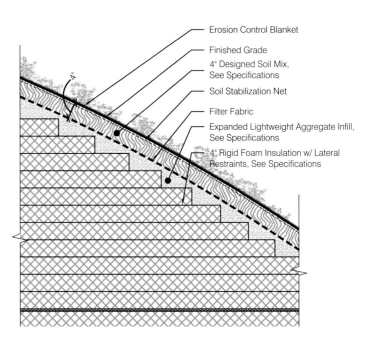

Erosion Control Blanket

Finished Grade

4" Designed Soil Mix, See Specifications

Soil Stabilization Net

Filter Fabric

Expanded Lightweight Aggregate Infill, See Specifications

4" Rigid Foam Insulation w/ Lateral Restraints, See Specifications

4"

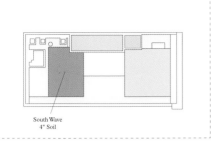

South Wave
4" Soil

P · Q · R

TOP: Placement of growing medium
onto south wave
BOTTOM LEFT: Prickly pear cactus on
the crest of the south wave
BOTTOM RIGHT: *Sedum lanceolatum*
exhumed by birds

Sedum telephioides
Allegheny stonecrop
A rare native that does well on exposed rock outcrops as well as gardens and landforms that are the analogs of the ASLA green roof's south wave on terra firma.

Sedum sexangulare
Watch chain sedum
A beautiful and tough sedum brings intricate texture to the plant palette and the reliability of a tried-and-true green roof plant (also planted on terrace).

Sedum stenopetalum
Worm leaf stonecrop
The seasonal transition from summer-green to winter-red foliage, punctuated by yellow floral blooms in mid summer, provides a distinct jagged texture year-round to the south wave.

Sedum album
"Murale"
White stonecrop
This drought-tolerant evergreen sedum forms a spreading mat of rounded leaves and stalks. It thrives in full sun, but tolerates a wide range of conditions. (also planted on north wave).

Sedum floriferum
"Weihenstephaner Gold"
Stonecrop
A low-growing sedum spreads trailing stems across the substrate surface, forming a dense groundcover in well-drained areas with full sun (also planted on north wave).

Sedum spurium "Voodoo"
Two-row stonecrop
The reddish foliage and strength of this sedum make it a good selection for the south wave with 4" media depth and predominantly succulent plant palette, adding a strong reddish carpet effect, punctuated by bright greens and silver greens.

Orostachys boehmeri
Sedum boehmeri
The conical arrange-ment of the flower spike and whorled silvery leaves add a curious texture to the low-growing sedum plant palette of the south wave.

Sempervivum tectorum
Hens and chicks
The "house leeks" are an ancient group of green roof plants, enriching the planting with horticultural allegory and providing a radiating texture to the plant palette.

OPPOSITE PAGE AND LEFT: South wave perennials and succulents; plant descriptions by Richard Hindle (MVVA) and Marcus de la fleur (CDF)

RIGHT, TOP TO BOTTOM: South wave after planting in May 2006; south wave in August, insufficient plant growth and widespread plant failures; south wave after replanting in September

P · Q · R

Opuntia humifusa
Prickly pear cactus
Thrives in full sun and very-well-drained dry soils and substrate; the showy yellow flower and unique form bring an untamed curiousness to the crest of the south wave.

Silene caroliniana
Wild pink
This species thrives in sandy to rocky soils in full sun with afternoon shade, similar to summer conditions found on the south wave, with its subtle north-facing slope.

Phlox subulata
Moss phlox
A vigorous, spreading, mat-forming phlox that thrives in well-drained soils with good sun exposure; tolerates rocky soils and hot areas; the abundant flowers offer a red-purple color to the rooftop palette.

North Wave

The north wave, with six inches of soil depth, provides two more inches of planting medium than the south wave and allows the testing of perennial plant material. CDF and MVVA drafted a mix of drought-tolerant prairie species, Great Plains species, high desert species, and chryptophytes. The resulting prairie-like appearance was intended to form a strong visual contrast to the low-growing succulents of the south wave that are more reminiscent of typical green roofs. The highest grasses and perennials are planted on the crest of the wave to be visible from the street. Tried and tested succulents from Europe complement the prairie mix.

Marcus de la fleur from CDF sees the sedum additions as a backup for the prairie plants: "There is no track record of prairie plants sustaining green roof vegetation without supplemental irrigation. Three weeks of drought may equate to total failure. Take Chicago City Hall, for instance. A number of prairie plants failed in the second year, leaving brown spots behind. The adjacent sedums were able to fill most of the bare spots by next season."

So far both sedums and perennials have established themselves in the first growing season and started to form a plant community. As expected, the succulents on the moister bottom part of the wave grew vigorously, whereas growth was more moderate at the dry crest. Only the plants along the vertical edges did not do well, and a narrow strip had to be replanted with the same hardy succulent mix that was used on the south wave. This may have been in part due to insufficient water reaching the edge from the oscillating sprinkler temporarily located in the middle of the wave. Moreover, it was speculated that the metal edges, when heated up by the sun, accelerated the desiccation of the adjacent substrate.

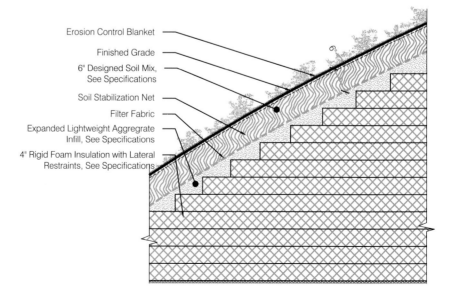

Erosion Control Blanket

Finished Grade

6" Designed Soil Mix,
See Specifications

Soil Stabilization Net

Filter Fabric

Expanded Lightweight Aggregrate
Infill, See Specifications

4" Rigid Foam Insulation with Lateral
Restraints, See Specifications

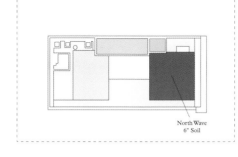

North Wave
6" Soil

North wave succulents; plant descriptions by Richard Hindle (MVVA) and Marcus de la fleur (CDF)

Delosperma nubigenum "Basutoland"
Ice plant
A fast-growing member of the green roof planting, this mat-forming succulent with showy flowers is well suited to rooftop conditions. Grows well in full sun and well-drained substrates (also planted on terraces).

Talinum calycinum
Fameflower
Well-suited to rocky soils and full sun; the beautiful purple flowers and slender succulent leaves are curious additions to the roof's terraces, adding a slight verticality to the terrace texture (also planted on terraces).

Sedum album "Murale"
White stonecrop
This drought-tolerant evergreen sedum forms a spreading mat of rounded leaves and stalks. It thrives in full sun, but tolerates a wide range of conditions (also planted on south wave).

Sedum floriferum "Weihenstephaner Gold"
Stonecrop
A low-growing sedum spreads trailing stems across the substrate surface, forming a dense groundcover in well-drained areas with full sun (also planted on south wave).

Sedum reflexum
Spruce-leaved stonecrop
A strong, low-growing plant forms a mat of gray-blue foliage and is well reputed for seeking out nooks and crannies in the garden, making it an excellent plant for coverage and filling tight areas (also planted on terraces).

Sedum spurium "Fuldaglut"
Two-Row stonecrop
The red, horizontally colonizing, foliage of this tough sedum break the homogeny of greens among the spurium-type ground covers. Full sun accentuates the red tips and pink floral displays of this Eurasian native (also planted on terraces).

Planting

P · Q · R

Eragrostis spectabilis
Purple lovegrass
The inflorescences of this low-growing grass bring a light, cloud-like texture with a hint of purple to the roof palette, and its tough foliage tolerates dry soils with low organic content in full sun.

Allium schoenoprasum
Chive
An incredible drought-tolerant bulb that brightens the north wave with reliable green foliage and large purple inflorescence that provides aesthetic and wildlife benefits.

Bouteloua gracilis
Blue grama grass
The unique inflorescence of this drought-tolerant grass is suspended horizontally from the tip of the flower stalk, bringing aesthetic interest to the roofs plant community.

Allium cernuum
Nodding onion
A native onion relative that dispays inflorescences on long stalks; plantings of this perennial bulb on the street side of the north wave ensures their visibilty from the street at ground level, as well as from the rooftop terraces.

Elymus virginicus
Virginia wild rye
A rugged eastern native rye grass inhabits varied soil types, thriving in full sun exposure.

Achillea millefolium
Yarrow
A vigorous "weed" whose cultivated relatives often outcompete many other species in the typical garden setting.

North wave perennials continued; plant descriptions by Richard Hindle (MVVA) and Marcus de la fleur (CDF)

Tradescantia bracteata
Spiderwort
The well-drained soils and exposure to full sun on the north wave are ideal for this spiderwort, whose purple flowers bring aesthetic interest to the green roof plant community.

Solidago nemoralis
Old field goldenrod
This conspicuous inhabitant of native fields colonizes and establishes itself readily. As it is easily recognized, it brings meadow analogies to the rooftop, serving a didactic and aesthetic purpose.

Artemisia ludoviciana
Silver king
The dusty silver foliage and erect habit of this grass add unique texture and color to the north wave meadow. This drought-tolerant plant is well suited to gravely soil and competitive meadow conditions.

Coreopsis verticillata
Thread-leaved tickseed
Numerous yellow blooms and vigorous growth characteristics make this well suited to the stresses of rooftop gardens.

Asclepias tuberosa
Butterfly milkweed
A showy native milkweed that thrives in dry soils with low organic content, offering a bright orange inflorescence to the roof's color pallette, it brings wildlife interest in addition to its ability to live among other strong plants.

Rudbeckia hirta
Black-eyed susan
Usually inhabits waste-places, roadsides, and dry fields, making the species well suited to harsh environments; it displays a large composite flower similar to its commonly cultivated relatives but with the strength of a wild native.

Planting

TOP: Incisions were made into the erosion mat in order to plant the plugs into the growing medium.
MIDDLE: North wave after planting in May 2006
BOTTOM: North wave in August: substantial plant growth occurred

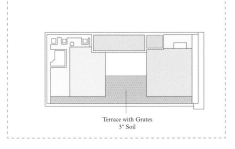

Terrace with Grates
3" Soil

BOTTOM LEFT: Grating edge condition
BOTTOM RIGHT: Fameflowers are starting to poke through the grates.

Terrace with Grates

The plants below the grating grow in three-inch-deep medium and consist of a mix of proven sedum species. From the top of the soil to the underside of the grate there is a clear space of about three inches for the plants. In the beginning there was a lot of concern about this novel planting condition. "The plants under the grating required selecting just the right kind of sedum for an environment that included a metal grate that would get hot in the sun, but only allows a certain amount of sunlight through. The sedums had to be tall enough to occasionally poke through, but not so tall that they would get trampled, or cooked by the grille," as Michael Van Valkenburgh pointed out, relating the concerns of CDF who initialized this solution.

The overheating problem was addressed by selecting aluminum as the grating material. As it turned out, this reflective metal with its low conductivity actually stayed cooler on hot summer days than adjacent surfaces like the wood deck. Also the lower light levels did not cause problems since the selected sedums tolerate part-shade conditions. In fact, the shading by the grates created a slightly cooler microclimate producing more benign conditions than on the fully exposed areas on the roof (see "Monitoring"). Not only did the planted succulents grow vigorously below the grates, unwanted volunteers like Siberian elm seedlings, grasses, and wood sorrel also took advantage of the favorable growing conditions (see "Maintenance").

The designers point out that the relative success of the shaded area below the grates is clearly dependant on a particular climate. It worked well in the extreme dry summer of Washington DC, but in a cooler climate with higher rainfall, results could be different and the same solution might result in conditions that are too moist for succulents.

Beyond performance issues, the design team sees a unique opportunity in the arrangement of plants growing through a grated walking surface. They hope that the plants, by their presence and their absence, will register the movement patterns of the visitors on the roof over time. Plants poking through the grate in heavy trafficked areas will get "haircuts" and regenerate (sedum easily regenerates from cuttings). In less frequented areas like corners, the plants will be undisturbed and visible above the grate.

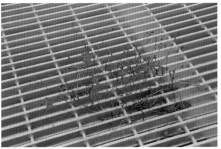

Sedum sexangulare
Watch chain sedum
A beautiful, and tough sedum brings intricate texture to the plant palette and the reliability of a tried-and-true green roof plant (also planted on the south wave).

Sedum kamtschaticum
Kamtschaticum sedum
A low-growing sedum spreads trailing stems across the substrate surface, forming a dense groundcover in well-drained areas with full sun.

Delosperma nubigenum "Basutoland"
Ice plant
A fast-growing member of the green roof planting, this mat-forming succulent with showy flowers is well suited to rooftop conditions. Grows well in full sun and well-drained substrates (also planted on north wave).

Talinum calycinum
Fameflower
Well-suited to rocky soils and full sun; the beautiful purple flowers and slender succulent leaves are curious additions to the roof's terraces, adding a slight verticality to the terrace texture (also planted on north wave).

Sedum reflexum
Spruce-leaved stonecrop
A strong, low-growing plant forms a mat of gray-blue foliage, and is well reputed for seeking out nooks and crannies in the garden, making it an excellent plant for coverage and filling tight areas (also planted on north wave).

Sedum spurium "John Creech" **Two-row stonecrop**
The diversity of habitats and locations in which this Eurasian sedum is found make it a good selection for the diversity of conditions across North America. It requires full sun to thrive and readily establishes itself in shallow substrate depths of 4 inches.

Sedum spurium "Fuldaglut"
Two-row stonecrop
This species of stonecrop tolerates a wide range of soil and light conditions, making it a reliable selection under the grates and on the exposed terraces (also planted on north wave).

Sedum spurium "White Form"
Two-row stonecrop
The vast geographic and climatic ranges colonized by this sedum and its tolerance for partial shade as well as full sun make it a versatile plant among taller perennials, sedums, and between the cracks of green roof architecture.

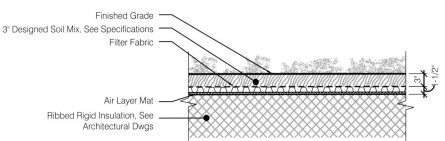

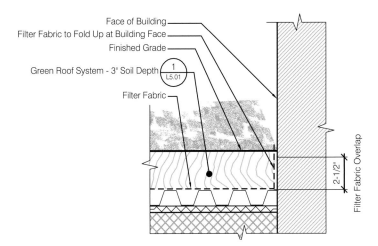

Planting

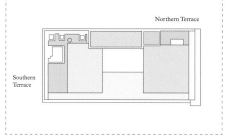

Terrace without Grates

Although all other areas of the terrace are planted with the same succulent mix as planted below the grates, drastic differences became apparent between the southern and the northern parts of the terrace after the first growing season. The plants on the southern part of the terrace remained small and compact, whereas the same plant mix established itself very quickly and doubled in size on the shadier northern terrace. Similar to the south wave, the lack of growth in the southern part was attributed to high temperatures (up to 136°F), high light levels, and infrequent watering (see "Monitoring").

Dried-out root balls, the result of inadequate watering, further inhibited the establishment of the plants. Nurseries customarily grow plugs in peat moss, which turns hydrophobic and will repel water if allowed to reach a stage where it is completely dried out. If this happens prior to the plant having driven roots into the surrounding soil, the plant is left in a dry pocket and begins to wither. When regular watering is hard to achieve during plant establishment, using an alternate planting method like spreading sedum cuttings (inexpensive, but slower establishment) can alleviate the problem.

In the current situation plant density will be increased on the south terrace by adding more sedums and watering them more evenly. The goal is to cover all exposed surfaces as soon as possible, effectively reducing the high temperatures in the immediate vicinity of the plants. As a second measurement a timer was added to the temporary sprinkler system to allow more frequent but shorter periods of watering.

Summary

The first growing season showed that the overall planting strategy of testing a variety of suitable indigenous plants backed by a system of successful green roof performers was well chosen. Most areas are in the preliminary stages of a thriving plant community, but there are also others (with thin soils and high light levels) that even overtaxed the hardiest succulents. Once more it was reaffirmed that continuous care and maintenance from the beginning is the key for successful plant establishment even (or especially) for the extensive sections of a green roof (see "Maintenance").

The varied depth of soil, the pronounced topography of the roof, and the building materials that were selected indeed created a multitude of growing environments with starkly differing microclimates. The roof has shown that a north-facing slope with six inches of growing substrate is radically different from a south-facing slope with two inches less. The ASLA roof experience confirmed that in extreme planting conditions (and roof surfaces clearly fall in that category), small deviations can make the difference between success and failure.

TOP ROW: Plant development on the northern terrace from May to August 2006

BOTTOM ROW: Inhibited plant development of the southern terrace from May to August; image to the right shows south terrace after replanting in September

P · Q · R

Roof Section

It is commonly said that the roof section represents the heart of every green roof project and that there are no two alike. This is also true for the ASLA roof. The current composition of layers is the result of teamwork between the landscape architects, the architect, the green roof manufacturer, and the structural engineer responding to the particular situation of the ASLA roof. Each member fed specific knowledge and concerns into the development process. The landscape architect and the architect synthesized the individual advice into a final product. The structural engineer continuously checked if all the components were within the load-bearing capacity of the roof (see "Load Capacity").

Before explaining the individual elements of the roof, one has to be aware of some of the specific conditions of this roof. The client and the design team did not select individual materials from various manufacturers, but used a complete system from one manufacturer. This means that all the components from the waterproofing to the growing medium came from a single source tailored to the specific design needs of the ASLA roof.

The advantage of using one system is that all the components are chemically compatible—a common concern when choosing materials from different manufacturers. The dis-advantage is that on an experimental roof like the ASLA only one system could be tested.

The second factor that has to be taken into account is that the ASLA roof serves as a nationwide demonstration project. Hence an enormous effort went into the prevention of any conceivable malfunction. In addition to its high visibility, the complex roof design created unique demands on green roof technology. As a result, the current roof section is an elaborate composition with ample safety reserves. Since all the material is donated, the reduction of all layers to the bare minimum was less a concern than providing the best growing conditions possible. These unique parameters have to be taken into account when studying the various layers of the ASLA roof.

1 4.5" depth extensive growing medium
2 Soil-stabilization net
3 Filter fabric
4 Lightweight aggregate
5 Rigid insulation
6 Galvanized-metal decking
7 Uplift mitigation cables
8 Steel wave structure
9 Galvanized steel handrail
10 Supplemental AC units and bathroom exhaust and intake
11 HVAC unit
12 Aluminum grating walking surface
13 Wood deck
14 Metal grating structure
15 Wood deck structure
16 3" depth extensive growing medium
17 Filter fabric
18 Water-retention and drainage mat
19 Aeration mat
20 Rigid insulation
21 Root barrier
22 Waterproof membrane
23 Dense deck
24 Bathroom exhaust and intake roof penetrations
25 HVAC roof penetrations
26 Metal decking roof
27 Structural connections points from wave to roof structure below
28 Relocated roof drain
29 Headquarters of the American Society of Landscape Architects
30 6" depth semi-intensive growing medium
31 Soil-stabilization net
32 Filter fabric
33 Lightweight aggregate
34 Rigid insulation
35 Uplift prevention cables
36 Steel wave structure
37 Galvanized-metal decking
38 HVAC unit
39 Wood deck
40 12" depth intensive growing medium
41 21" depth intensive growing medium
42 Filter fabric
43 Moisture-retention and drainage mat
44 Rigid insulation
45 Root protection barrier
46 Waterproof membrane
47 Aperture
48 Drainage scupper
49 Elevator shaft extension
50 Galvanized-steel trellis
51 New CMU stair tower extension building
52 Fire-rated glass door
53 New staircase
54 Existing elevator shaft
55 HVAC roof penetration
56 Relocated roof drain

See p. 114–119 for items in green.

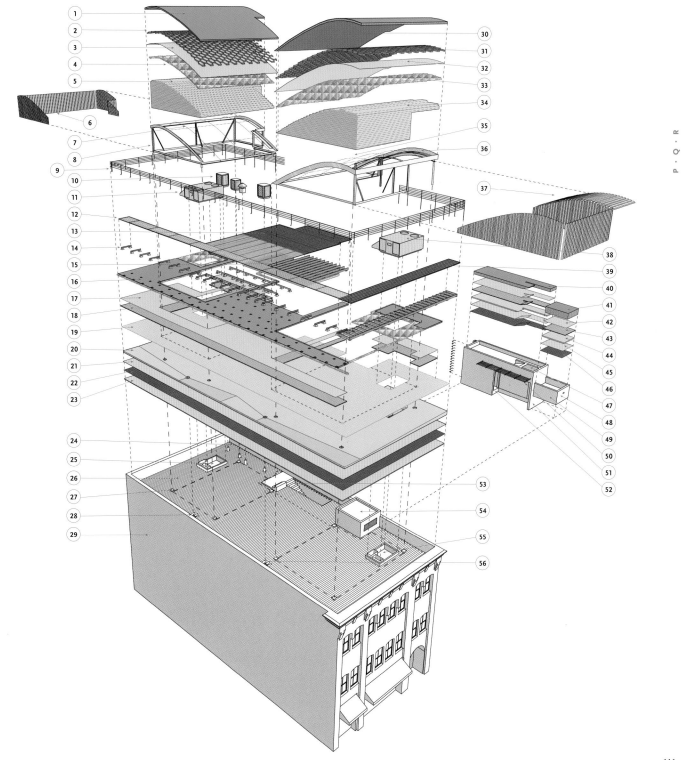

Roer Section

Waterproofing

The former ASLA roof consisted of a metal deck overlaid with an insulation layer and covered by a PVC waterproofing membrane. For the retrofit, the design team decided to build up the roof differently. The water-proofing membrane and insulation were stripped off from the existing metal decking. The steel deck was then overlaid with a dense decking consisting of gypsum boards.
The dense decking was coated with a new waterproof membrane composed of hot rubberized asphalt with fabric reinforcement. The hot fluid (up to 375 degrees Fahrenheit) was applied in two coats, amounting to a total thickness of about a quarter inch.
The new membrane adheres directly to the dense decking and forms a monolithic layer without any seams.

Root Barrier

The asphalt waterproofing itself is not classified as root resistant and had to be reinforced with a root barrier. This barrier consists of rubberized asphalt enforced with polyester and treated with a root-repelling agent. It was rolled out and embedded into the waterproofing while it was still warm. The eighth-inch-thick sheets overlap at the seams and are torch welded.

It should be noted that there are also synthetic waterproofing membranes (like PVC liners) available that are root resistant and do not require an additional root barrier.

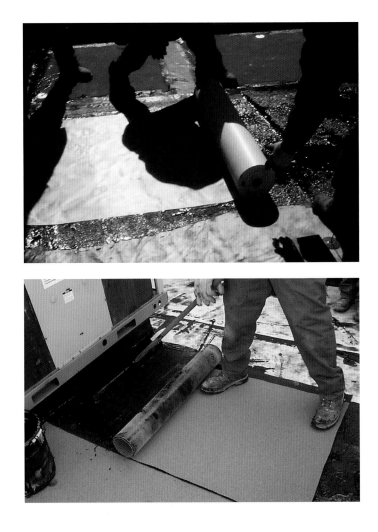

Tapered insulation covering
the whole roof was laid on top
of the root barrier.

Insulation

The root barrier was then overlaid with insulation boards made of extruded polystyrene that has high water resistance and compressive strength (see "Insulation"). The insulation boards were cut in wedge shapes to create a two-percent cross slope over the whole roof (see "Drainage").

Up to this point, the roof system is, with the exception of the root barrier, not any different from any other regular roof application. The main difference from the old roof is that now the insulation layer is placed above the waterproofing membrane, whereas on the previous roof the insulation was located below the waterproofing. This so-called Inverted Roof Membrane Assembly (IRMA) is a common roof type for green roof applications. It has the advantage that the boards of the insulation layer protect the waterproofing membrane from injury during and after construction and from the corrosive effect of the elements.[6]

At the ASLA roof, the scope for the architect ended with the insulation layer and the landscape architect was responsible for the systems above it. This separation follows the typical pattern of the architect being responsible for the waterproofing and insulation of the building, and the landscape architect for components enabling plant growth above the insulation.

A quarter-inch-thick aeration and drain mat was laid on top of the insulation.

Aeration and Drainage Mat

The sloping plane of the insulation layer was entirely overlaid with an aeration and drainage mat that creates a quarter-inch-wide airspace. Although most of the rainwater is held and drained by another drain mat directly below the growing medium, some water and moisture will percolate down to the waterproofing and insulation. Standing water decreases the overall insulation capacity of the roof. Thus an aeration layer is necessary to enhance airflow and to dry out the insulation after a heavy rainfall. Only below the waves, the aeration mat also serves as a drain mat and carries water from higher-lying roof areas to the inlets (see "Drainage").

Water-Retention and Drainage Mat

In all planting areas except the waves, the aeration mat was overlaid with another larger water-retention and drainage mat. The ASLA roof pitches about two percent from west to east and the drain mat ensures that water percolating down from the growing substrate is either stored or drained. The mat is one-inch thick and egg crate–shaped. The egg crates serve as a water reservoir that plant roots can tap into. Once the cups are filled, excess water will overflow to the internal drains at the east side of the building (see "Drainage").

At the deeper sections over the stair tower (twelve inches) and elevator shaft (twenty-four inches), the mat is thicker (two and a half inches) and its cups are filled with expanded shale (forty-five percent shale and fifty-five percent air) that delays the dehydration of the reservoir and maintains a more stable moisture regimen.

The planting areas of the waves did not receive a combined retention and drainage layer because the cups do not hold water in sloping conditions. On the waves, a simple drainage mat (the same as the aeration mat) carries excess water down the slope.

Filter fabric was laid over the retention and drainage mats.

Filter Fabric

The water-retention and drainage layer was overlaid with a filter fabric that separates it from the growing medium above. Only roots that will tap into the water storage layer below will penetrate the fabric.

P · Q · R

Growing Medium

The growing medium as the top layer provides nutrients and structure for the roots to anchor in. The proprietary mixes of the manufacturer consist of a lightweight aggregate, expanded shale, and some compost. The organic components make up about three to six percent of the shallow planting areas. Two different mixes were applied based on the thickness of the planting area. The mix for deeper planting areas (twelve inches and twenty-four inches) has slightly more organics (from six to twelve percent) and a higher number of fines. This mix is also heavier and allows a higher water-holding capacity in order to support the larger plants of these areas (see "Planting").

It has to be noted that any romantic notion of natural soil formation is misplaced when it comes to green roofs. As is common for green roofs, the growing medium of the ASLA roof is a tightly controlled manufactured blend, consisting of independently occurring ingredients and composed according to the individual design philosophy and experiences of the manufacturer. As in winemaking or cooking, there are many different approaches and nuances for soil-making as well. Depending on the design goals and weight limits, mixes can range from oven-baked expanded aggregates to volcanic rocks, to recycled brick, or locally available soils.

Conclusion

In conclusion, one has to realize that there is (as in any other complex project) no cookie cutter approach when it comes to the design of a green roof section. Though certain layers are always present—water-proofing, root barrier (if waterproofing is not root resistant), insulation (if above waterproofing), protection layer, drainage layer, separation layer, and the growing medium—their actual composition varies widely responding to a particular situation. The current ASLA roof composition is just one possible scenario amongst many; a different design team might have come up with a very different layer composition. In the end each individual green-roof project has to find its own appropriate composition.

Schedule

Spontaneous Vegetation

The project took nineteen months from initiation to completion. It started with a structural feasibility study in September 2004, the design process began in April 2005, the project was sent out for bid in September 2005, and was completed at the end of April in 2006.

A much-discussed idea by the team and the client was to include areas of self-colonization on the roof for study purposes. Spontaneous vegetation was used in early green roof designs (by Le Corbusier and Atelier 5, for example) and appears today in a series of projects in the UK and Switzerland that recreate on the roof habitat that is lost on the ground.[7] Initially MVVA proposed to leave one of the waves bare for seedlings brought by wind and birds. Later, the deeper section of the staircase shaft was taken into consideration. In the end, the team abandoned the idea. They were concerned that mixing a spontaneous vegetation plot with purposefully planted plots at this small scale would not keep these two vegetation types separate.

Besides this imminent maintenance problem, MVVA speculated that the spontaneous colonization of the prominent staircase shaft could create negative associations of neglect. David Yocca from CDF finally argued that this prominent plant location should not be given over to volunteer vegetation and concluded that "the idea of spontaneous vegetation is a worthy pursuit, but unfortunately, it just doesn't work in this design." The green roof task force finally agreed to omit passive planting concepts from the project (see "Maintenance" and "Planting").

Stair Tower

TOP: The arrival sequence is structured into four phases. (plan by MVVA)
BOTTOM: 3D studies of entrance sequence (by MVVA)

The stair tower replaces the two previous maintenance hatches and ladders with a convenient stair that leads up to the roof. The tower is a continuation of the stair system in the building, erected directly over existing steel trusses. It is built in a simple utilitarian style with gray CMU blocks and a neutral white interior matching the rest of the stair house.

The designers emphasize that the tower layout is the result of a well-calculated arrival sequence. In fact, the entrance is characterized by a gradual revelation of the roof. When ascending the long and narrow staircase from below, one can already catch a glimpse of daylight reflecting on the top wall (1). After having arrived at the top of the stairs, one has to turn around and is then faced with a view of a narrow loggia (2), lit indirectly from the side and directly from above by a skylight sending the sun's rays down the interior north wall (see "Aperture"). The skylight at the end reveals a little abstract rectangle of blue sky, but will at some point show the green or red of the grown-up flame sumacs planted behind (3) (see "Planting").

When advancing a few more steps, the wood deck and parts of the north wave are further revealed, heightening the sense of arrival. After walking through the glass door, entering the deck, and turning another ninety degrees right, the massive waves to the left and right direct and frame the views to the panorama of other roofs, facades, and towers over Washington (4).

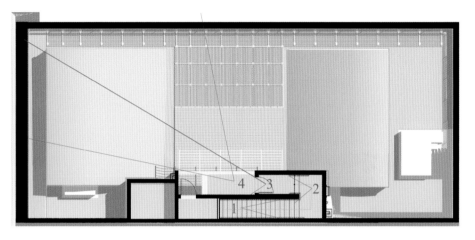

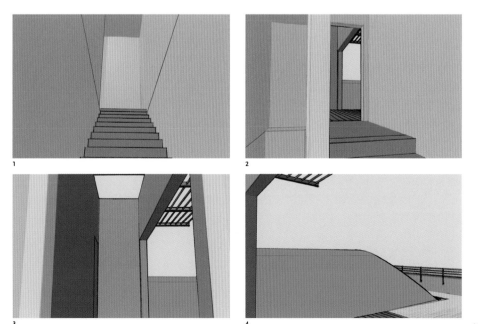

1

2

3

4

Stair Tower

S · T

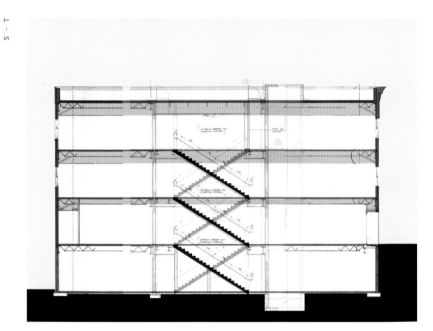

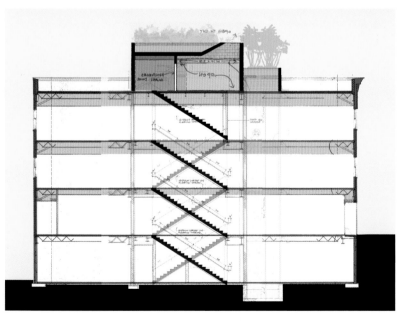

Visibility

The client wanted to ensure that the crest of the north wave would be visible from the street level. 3D modeling was used to determine the effect and led to an increase of the height of the north wave during the design process.

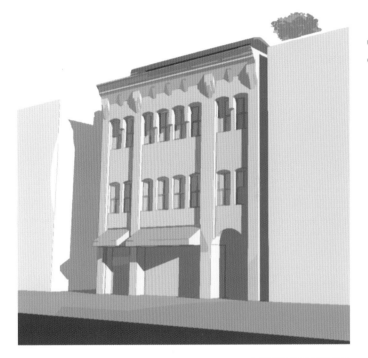

Waves

The two waves were filled with insulation boards (see "Insulation"), because filling the waves with soil would have by far exceeded the load capacity of the roof. The side walls of the waves were clad with metal decking tilted vertically. The metal decking was initially the choice of the structural engineer to contain the foam. The structural device was meant to be covered with another more decorative material. At the end, the designers decided to use the decking as the primary layer to stay consistent with the industrial materials of the roof. Earlier in the design process, glass side panels, to reveal the insides of the waves, were discussed, but this idea was dropped for cost reasons.

The structural integrity of the two waves created a unique problem. The waves had to be shielded from lateral pressures and securely tied down to the roof structure to resist uplift from wind passing over the buildings and prevent it from waving like an airfoil. The structural engineers from RSA and the landscape architects from MVVA developed a curved steel frame tied down to the roof structure at discrete points with several cables running over the rigid insulation and metal decking side panels.

The eleven-inch-wide curved steel plates serve not only as connectors for the structural steel cables but also have embedded connections that the slope-stabilization net attaches to (see "Erosion"). The plates further function as landscape edging, containing the growing medium of the planting area above. Weepholes release excess water coming down from the soil. Jeannette Laramee, project manager from RSA, describes the design process as a highly collaborative effort: "It was a forum in which neither of us was used to working; we were part structural engineers, part architect, they were landscape architects trying to understand steel design. Communication and diligence by both parties was critical, and the end result was a structural design that not only served to effectively mitigate the effects of wind uplift, but also was a solution which became a key architectural element."

The designers point out that the tops of the waves are held level, whereas the whole deck and grating is sloping. The waves create a "perfect horizon" for viewers looking up against the level facades of the surrounding buildings, effectively countering the sloping plane of the wood deck and grating.

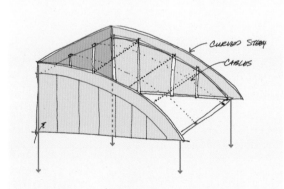

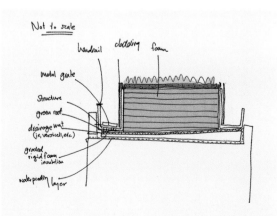

TOP: The structural support frame of the waves is only connected via discrete points (black dots) to the building in order to keep perforation of the waterproofing membrane to a minimum (drawing by MVVA).

BOTTOM: Weepholes along the back side frame of the north wave release the excess water of the future planting areas.

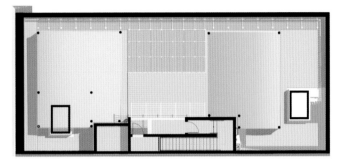

U · V · W

U · V · W

1

2

3

4

5

6

7

8

9

Construction sequence:
1: Point connections to steel truss system of existing roof structure
2–5: Erection of wave frames
6–10: Cladding of steel frames
11: Build-up of roof layers
12: Filling of waves with insulation boards

13: Spread of lightweight aggregate infill
14: Installation of tie-down steel cables
15–16: Filling of soil-stabilization net with growing medium
17: Planting through erosion mat
18: Finished north wave

10

11

12

13

14

15

16

17

18

Notes

1   For example, the German landscape architect Peter Latz was one of the first to propose granular substrates with minimal organic content—a technique that is commonly used in green roof technology today.

2   In Germany, which has slightly less rainfall than Washington DC, green roofs with four inches of substrate are expected to retain seventy percent of the rainfall (DIN1986-2).

3   Barbara Deutsch and Heather Whitlow, "Re-greening Washington DC: A Green Roof Vision Based on Quantifiying Stormwater and Air Quality Benefits," paper submitted for: Greening Rooftops for Sustainable Communities, conference, Washington DC, (2005).

4   Ed Snodgrass, "100 Extensive Green Roofs: Lessons Learned," paper submitted for: Greening Rooftops for Sustainable Communities, conference, Washington DC, (2005).

5   Ibid.; Bradley Rowe, "Evaluation of Sedum and Michigan Native Taxa for Green Roof Applications," paper submitted for: Greening Rooftops for Sustainable Communities, conference, Washington DC, (2005); Paul Kephart, "Living Architecture: An Ecological Approach," paper submitted for: Greening Rooftops for Sustainable Communities, conference, Washington DC, (2005).

6   In conventional inverted roofs the insulation boards are typically held in place by a ballast layer of gravel or river stones. In green roof applications the stone ballast is exchanged for the growing medium for the plants. This is actually how green roof research started in Europe.

7   Stephan Brenneisen, "Biodiversity of European Greenroofs," paper submitted for Greening Rooftops for Sustainable Communities conference, Chicago, (2003), 323–29; Dusty Gedge and Mathew Frith, "An Eye for the Green Top: An Independent Voice for Green Roofs in the UK," paper submitted for: Greening Rooftops for Sustainable Communities, conference, Washington DC, (2005).

Part IV: Interview

Christian Werthmann talks with
Michael Van Valkenburgh

CW: The vast majority of roof space in the United States is mostly used to house mechanical equipment. By employing modern green roof technology your team converted one of these deserted roofs into an amenity for the inhabitants of the building. Is this the beginning of a new trend?

MVV: Air-handlers and other mechanical equipment are experienced as hostile things when you find them on a roof, which means that nobody wants to be around them. As a result, there has been, in recent memory, little investment in creating a welcoming rooftop environment. In the end, a trend toward untapped environmental advantages of green roofs might in some ways be secondary to trends that recognize their experiential potential. As we have worked on the ASLA headquarters, the driver of the design has been the environmental amenity of the green roof, with an eye toward also making a place that's good for inhabitation. Simply stated: if you go up on a roof and start putting plants there, and you start making it attractive, I think people's reaction is going to be: "Oh my god, this whole other amenity is possible." This leads me to wonder how for so many years people allowed the machines to take over.

CW: Where do you see the biggest field of application in our built environment for an accessible green roof like the ASLA headquarters? Is it the office building in a downtown location?

MVV: I think so, yes. The ASLA green roof is all about being in this dense, challenged urban neighborhood and the oasis the green roof offers.

CW: Are green roofs and roof gardens then related to urban density? Will they diminish with the further expansion of suburbia?

MVV: There will probably be green roofs in the suburbs, but not for the obvious density reasons that your question acknowledges. The inhabitation of roofs is going to be related to the environmental gain of the green roof. The reduced energy consumption and also temperature mitigation of storm-water runoff from roofs are certainly issues in suburbia, and in many instances, suburban development is in closer proximity to more fragile ecosystems. In Alumnae Valley at Wellesley College, for example, our Cattail Marsh functions to reduce the temperature of the roof runoff that's from the surrounding parking structures and new campus center. That temperature reduction could have been achieved with a green roof, and this is where limitations start to become relevant factors in suburban projects. The limits on development related to ecological and environmental regulations are significant, and a green roof can help tremendously in that regard.

CW: Do you think that the ASLA green roof was built because the ASLA as an institution just wanted it?

MVV: It was inspired by concern for the local watershed—some people in Washington feel that if there were a radical green roof movement there, the degraded water quality of the Anacostia River could be improved. In cities that have proximity to difficult hydrologies, like the Anacostia, the water quality could conceivably be improved in a measurable way. As a contrast, the sheer volume of water in the Hudson River would make the impact of a green roof program in Manhattan harder to assess. It still might be important, but it would be difficult to measure.

CW: The hydrological issue arises in a lot of other American cities; many have flooding problems and water-quality issues.

MVV: This is an aside, but I think a relevant one. Our office in New York plays volleyball on a pier in the Hudson River every Wednesday. We were playing one night during a violent cloudburst, and the Hudson River, which is enormous, was noticeably surcharged in its depth by that storm. It was frightening how fast the river level increased because of that runoff; we were wondering, "Are we okay out here?" It was literally rising that quickly. We observed firsthand the tremendous amount of uncontrolled run-off that a major city creates and the difficulty that it creates for even a very large river.

CW: The retrofit of the small ASLA roof was not inexpensive. Although half of the cost lies in making the roof accessible, it still could be prohibitive for other clients.

MVV: That's a good point. This is an area where research in business schools could go a long way toward recognizing the return on the investment. For instance, how do you measure productivity related to the quality of the work environment? If one had to justify investing in more outdoor space in pure market terms, I think it could be quantified and defended.

I don't know much about the commercial real estate market, but in the private market, in the business of co-ops and condominiums, there is a huge property value added by having accessible outdoor space. I suppose if everybody had all of this space, it might diminish its value, but short term, I think there is actually great real estate value in having these areas. For instance, I think fifty or sixty people work in the ASLA building—people who now have access to outdoor space.

CW: When faced with the limited load capacities of the roof, you started talking about creating a hybrid between a green roof and a roof garden. Can you explain the most important aspects and advantages of this hybrid?

MVV: The typical sedum mat contributes to environmental health, but visually it is very banal, and what we're creating with ASLA is something that has more range, but doesn't stray too far off the ranch. In other words, by taking on a slightly higher burden of maintenance, one gets a significantly higher-value landscape experience.

New York sidewalks served as an
inspiration for the grating design
(by MVVA staff).

1. TRANSPARENT FROM ONE SIDE, SOLID FROM THE OTHER
2. HAS A SENSE OF DIRECTIONALITY - THAT COULD WORK WELL
   WITH WAVES & WOOD DECKING
3. VERY STRONG (LOW DEFLECTION)
4. COULD TURN PANELS FOR DIFFERENT LIGHT/PLANT
   EXPERIMENTS

I SAW THIS ON THE WAY TO WORK
TODAY & MADE ME WANT TO RECONSIDER
BAR GRATING

CW: What about the combination of the sedum mat plus the steel grill that you can walk on? It seems to me this combination is the true expression of the hybrid.

MVV: Yes, the grill over the sedum mat seems to provide all the environmental usefulness of the sedum mat with the added advantage of providing access. It accommodates cleaning and retention of water, plus you can walk on some parts of it. For me, that was a big breakthrough. I haven't seen it in any other design so far, but we had to battle with the high-heels issue. To counter this, we also have a wood deck with a level change, something solid that people are clearly invited to walk on. The mix of materials is quite beautiful.

CW: I found it interesting that the design team decided against structural reinforcement of the roof and accepted the given load limits. Was it a decision to stay financially feasible?

MVV: No, it was mostly because the client group, led by Dennis Carmichael of EDAW, wisely maintained the position that we need to stay within such limitations so that the demonstration green roof doesn't become inaccessible to others because of cost.

CW: Speaking of costs, was there at any time the thought of saving costs by leaving the air handlers in place?

MVV: There was quite a lot of pressure to do that. Again, Dennis identified these as limitations that every roof faces. But it reaches a point of absurdity on this very small roof, with these obnoxious airhandlers right in the middle of the space. It is easy to romanticize certain things about urban life, but extreme mechanical noise is one that is difficult to have a sense of humor about. So the objection to them is not what they look like, but rather the noise they generated right in the middle of this garden. That is why we relocated them behind the waves.

CW: The design team took great care to choreograph a successful entrance to the garden. Can you describe the most important aspects of this entrance sequence?

MVV: Well, in all landscapes, how the experience of the spaces unfolds, whether it's with fluidity or not, is always a primary concern of mine. So when you open the door to the roof and are immediately presented with the continuous surface—the waves that the two landforms and the grill with the planting in the middle make—you're held there because you're perpendicular to the spine of the waves; you're held by the first experience. Also, the stairs are lined up to look at the one really redeeming thing in the larger landscape, which is the beautiful tower of the synagogue across the way.

CW: In the design discussions, numerous references were made to precedents like the High Line in New York, the roof gardens of Le Corbusier and Burle Marx.

Early design exploration of the
perspectival effect of the waves
(by MVVA)

Are any ideas from those examples present in the current design? And how much do you value precedents in your work?

MVV: There is less of a direct connection with Burle Marx, although through Roberto's work, we were freed as designers to appreciate and reflect on the sensuality of landscape. The waves as forms, although not explicitly traceable to anything by Burle Marx, are an instance of that sensuality.

The actual form, as you know, comes from a Corbusier roof [Villa Immeuble in Paris]. Corbusier used the rounded form of the skylights as a screening device that also referenced the notion of an abstracted landscape, a mountain form. So that's an explicit reference, although I have to say that the idea of the topography was from an even simpler idea.

We were sitting around in the beginning of the project saying, "How does anyone start a design?" Such an interesting thing, but not something you could write a set of rules for. My design processes are not driven by, but are activated by, imagining the use—by asking the simple question of what a bodily experience here is going to be. John on the design team said, "You know, if I went up there, I'd sit over here; I would want to be tilted up—I would come here and work on my tan." Not surprised that he would say that—the model in the group! But when he said that, I had this notion. Simply put, it was the act of thinking of a body propped up slightly on a landform, and the sense that if we activate the topography of the roof, it would be amazing.

CW: You said something about the use of the space. How do you expect people to use the roof?

MVV: We're planning on movable chairs for seating that are usable in the interstitial space between the two peaks of the wave.

TOP LEFT: Sod over a barrel-vaulted roof creates an artificial horizon in "Villa Immeuble," Le Corbusier's apartment in Paris (colored by MVVA).

TOP RIGHT: Early study of the north wave manipulating the urban context (by MVVA)

BOTTOM: Section of Villa Immeuble depicting soil on barrel roof (soil section colored by author)

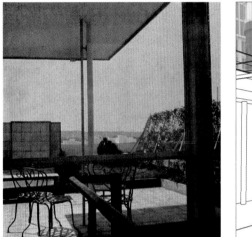

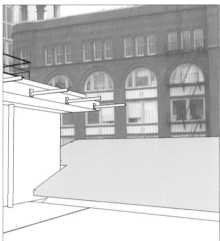

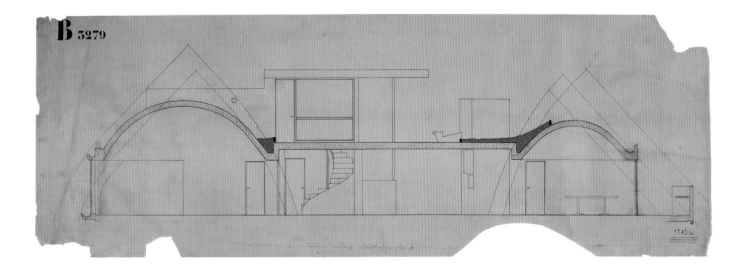

CW: Do you think people will use it for a coffee break or lunchtime?

MVV: I'm hoping that they will take their lunch there from time to time. We have this little garden at the office, and it's got just a couple of chairs in it. It's not the same people every day, but it is used. I love it when I get the chance to use it, even for a short period of time while I'm working. It's very calming.

CW: Let's talk about the relation of architecture and green roof. Is the roof garden independent of the style of a building? Did the retro style of the brownstone building of the ASLA headquarters influence your design in any way?

MVV: The style of the building didn't really influence the design, although we did want the front wave high enough for the plants to be visible from the street as a kind of signal.

CW: It wouldn't have mattered to you if the facade were steel/glass or brownstone?

MVV: No, I don't think so. I have an attitude about the relationship between landscape and architecture that some architects, I think, perceive as irreverence to their buildings. I don't mean it to be taken that way, but I feel that once you're outside the limits of a building, anything goes.

This notion that landscape and architecture are designed with a single, conceptual sweep, while a very beautiful idea, with extremely inspired applications—Kiley's Miller Garden is fantastic that way—is somewhat limiting. There are a thousand other much more surprising collisions, you know? I like the idea of a roof not being coordinated with the architecture—certainly not thoughtlessly applied without considering the impact of the roof garden on the architecture—but also the roof garden not being derivative, or at least always derivative, of some architectural concept. The landscape becomes its own integrity that's not sycophantic to the architecture—it stands on its own.

CW: Do you sometimes alter the design of buildings for your landscape purposes?

MVV: Oh yes, on multiple occasions. At the Vera List Courtyard at the New School, for instance, we extended the courtyard into the landscape for the purpose of structuring that experience. At the ASLA green roof—which, by the way, has an incredibly small architectural component—the primary architectural issues were the organization of the stair and door sequence to achieve the best "borrowed landscape" view when you leave the stair and go onto the roof.

CW: For the ASLA roof, you are proactive because you control the architectural part.

MVV: We've been proactive there. We asked to have the architect as our subcontractor and then we told them, "This is your shot—this has to be a really good thing." They have been really supportive.

CW: How was the process? Did you say, "We need access up there and this is how big it should be," and they worked out the details, or did they come up with where the staircase should be?

MVV: No; we did all of that.

CW: You stress that MVVA does not take a top-down approach when it comes to design, but seeks collaboration. In the ASLA roof garden, you were teamed up with another renowned firm, Conservation Design Forum (CDF). How did the design process work out with CDF?

MVV: CDF were our subconsultants, and although they participated in the overall design process, for the most part they reacted to what we did from a technical perspective. Their creative contribution had primarily to do with vegetation and also with the idea of the metal grate network with sedum growing through it—an idea, by the way, that I think is brilliant. We are very happy with their part of this project.

CW: Can you talk about the notion of the wild versus the controlled in your designs?

MVV: Every design comes down to striking the right balance, or tension, between wild and controlled. A little control goes a long way in a landscape. Control—which brings a strong clarity and graphic quality to work, makes for good pictures, but the landscape should be rich with experience, and so I am a little saddened by overly controlled landscapes—sort of like food that looks better than it tastes. There is of course great power to utilizing some control in landscape-making. The essence of this idea is at Woodland Cemetery, where Asplund puts a straight path right through a grove of trees that irregularly scamper around the straight lines. The tension between the ordering of the path and the disorder of trees plays out so beautifully—not unlike similar balances that most of us play out in our daily lives.

CW: I wonder how much influence landscape architects will have on green roof development in the United States. In Germany, about eighty-five percent of all green roofs are built without the involvement of a landscape architect. Green roofs are treated as technical applications that can be handled by the manufacturer. What can and should landscape architects contribute to the American green roof movement?

MVV: I am sure that we will end up with similar odds, and there is probably nothing wrong with that. Architects have even less favorable odds when it comes to how many new standard roofs they have a hand in shaping. Let me repeat something Martha Schwartz likes to say. If a landscape architect is going to be involved in a project, the difference better be apparent. Furthermore, that difference has to take into account the experiences the roofscape provides for inhabitation, whether it's how the roof looks from afar or the moment of peace it provides an office worker when he or she slips up the stairs to have a cup of tea. That's really the defining measure of its success.

CW: What about technical innovation? Will landscape architects play a role?

MVV: When we saw the RFP [Request for Proposal] for the ASLA green roof, we jumped at the chance to provide the lead, partly so we could participate in an effort to demonstrate how our profession can simultaneously be frugal and make a great difference through design—through a design that embraces the technical challenges as opening doors to design, not imposing limitations on it. We at MVVA have always been interested in technological innovation and the interface of this with design, for instance the emergence of tectonics in architecture and the exciting things we are seeing in the work of architects like the American James Carpenter and Behnisch and Behnisch in Germany.

CW: In the beginning of the design process you were not so sure if the project could produce an admiring gasp from a visitor. How about today?

MVV: I think my word was "wow," not "gasp," but either way! The rolling enclosure of the waves is going to feel really good when you sit on a bench or a chair. I guess that not everyone who goes up there will say "wow," but there may be quite a few smiles.

AFTERWORD

The ASLA green roof was conceived as a demonstration project—to encourage and advocate the use of green roofs for their environmental benefits and to showcase what landscape architects bring to this type of project. Since the roof was completed in April 2006, the response has been tremendous. Tours of and presentations on the roof have become routine, with requests coming in from landscape architects, architecture and engineering firms, public officials, the media, and the general public. Student groups have ranged from middle school and high school science and social studies classes, to undergraduate and graduate classes in landscape architecture, civil engineering, and environmental science. The extraordinary level of interest reflects both the uniqueness of the design and heightened public recognition of the need for solutions to our cities' growing environmental problems.

Like so many cities in the United States, Washington DC, faces serious water- and air-quality issues. Of DC's fifty-seven square miles, forty-six percent is covered with impervious surfaces. Nationwide, impervious surfaces are increasing at the rate of three percent per year. Green spaces are at a premium. Roofs, on the other hand, account for fifteen to twenty-five percent of land surface in cities. There is a significant body of research on the environmental benefits of green roofs, but there are not many green roofs outside of academic settings that are both monitored and accessible. And, since green roofs are still relatively new in the United States, there is a great demand for successful local examples. Building owners and developers want to know that these projects are feasible and marketable. Public officials and regulatory authorities want to know that they will deliver the promised benefits. ASLA's roof—and this book—are helping to fill that gap.

The value of ASLA's green roof as a demonstration project should only increase over time. The Society is committed to long-term monitoring, and storm-water retention and plant growth will continue to be tracked. Water-quality testing has also started. Sensors are in place on ASLA's and a neighbor's roof for temperature comparisons during the summer months. Part of the building storefront is being converted to house an exhibit on the roof, to complement the ongoing tours and lectures. With the support of a grant from the National Endowment for the Arts, a web-based "virtual" tour is in development, along with a workbook and discovery program for middle school students.

The value of the roof as an amenity will also increase over time as the plants mature. But, thanks to MVVA's design, it has already exceeded expectations as a usable, enjoyable space. Visitors almost always express surprise at how inviting and "not roof-like" the space is. In nice weather, the roof has even become popular as a venue for small receptions. Although the "public" use of the roof has so far taken priority over staff use of the space, staff are definitely enjoying the roof—and the public interest in it. Some staff members are also pitching in as volunteers for occasional weeding and to give tours and presentations.

For the promise of green roofs to be realized, they must become the rule rather than the exception. It will take time to reach that goal, but the response to the ASLA roof has been encouraging—as has the general increase in public discussion of green building and environmental issues. As the ASLA roof so powerfully shows, landscape architects have much to contribute to that dialogue.

Nancy C. Somerville
Executive Vice President/CEO
American Society of Landscape Architects

CONSTRUCTION DOCUMENTS

LAYOUT PLAN

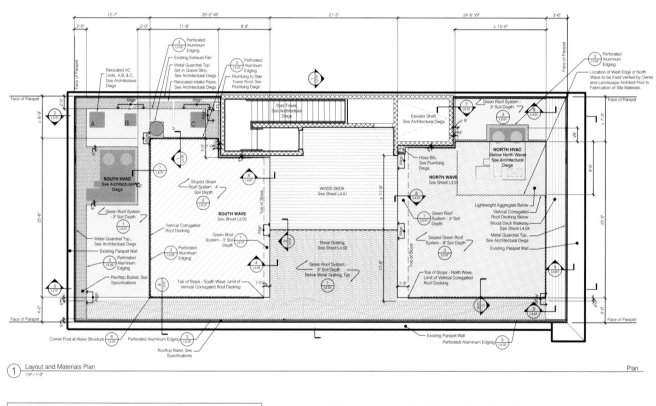

1 Layout and Materials Plan
1/4" = 1'-0"

Plan

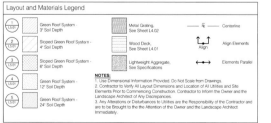

Layout and Materials Legend

1	Green Roof System - 3" Soil Depth	
2	Sloped Green Roof System - 4" Soil Depth	
3	Sloped Green Roof System - 6" Soil Depth	
4	Green Roof System - 12" Soil Depth	
5	Green Roof System - 24" Soil Depth	

Metal Grating, See Sheet L4.02

Wood Deck, See Sheet L4.01

Lightweight Aggregate, See Specifications

℄ Centerline

Align Elements

Elements Parallel

NOTES:
1. Use Dimensional Information Provided. Do Not Scale from Drawings.
2. Contractor to Verify All Layout Dimensions and Location of All Utilities and Site Elements Prior to Commencing Construction. Contractor to Inform the Owner and the Landscape Architect of Any Discrepancies.
3. Any Alterations or Disturbances to Utilities are the Responsibility of the Contractor and are to be Brought to the the Attention of the Owner and the Landscape Architect Immediately.

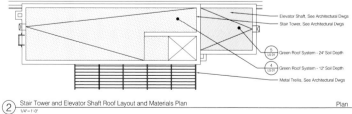

Elevator Shaft, See Architectural Dwgs
Stair Tower, See Architectural Dwgs
Green Roof System - 24" Soil Depth
Green Roof System - 12" Soil Depth
Metal Trellis, See Architectural Dwgs

2 Stair Tower and Elevator Shaft Roof Layout and Materials Plan
1/4" = 1'-0"

Plan

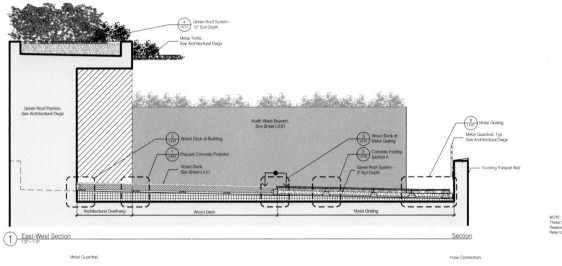

1 East-West Section
1/2" = 1'-0"

Section

Green Roof System - 12" Soil Depth
④ L5.01

Metal Trellis, See Architectural Dwgs

Green Roof Pavilion, See Architectural Dwgs

North Wave Beyond, See Sheet L3.01

⑤ L4.07 Wood Deck at Building

① L4.01 Precast Concrete Pedestal

Wood Deck, See Sheet L4.01

③ L4.01 Wood Deck at Metal Grating

② L4.03 Concrete Footing Section A

Green Roof System - 3" Soil Depth

⑧ L5.01 Metal Grating

Metal Guardrail, Typ. See Architectural Dwgs

Existing Parapet Wall

Architectural Overhang

Wood Deck

Metal Grating

NOTE:
These Sections are for Reference Only to show Relative Relationships between Site Elements. Refer to Details as noted.

Metal Guardrail,

Hose Connection,

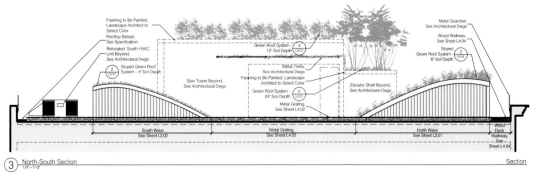

3 North-South Section
1/4" = 1'-0"

Section

Flashing to Be Painted, Landscape Architect to Select Color

Rooftop Ballast, See Specification

Relocated South HVAC Unit Beyond, See Architectural Dwgs

② L5.01 Sloped Green Roof System - 4" Soil Depth

Stair Tower Beyond, See Architectural Dwgs

④ L5.01 Green Roof System - 12" Soil Depth

Metal Trellis, See Architectural Dwgs

Flashing to Be Painted, Landscape Architect to Select Color

⑤ L5.01 Green Roof System - 24" Soil Depth

Metal Grating, See Sheet L4.02

Elevator Shaft Beyond, See Architectural Dwgs

Metal Guardrail, See Architectural Dwgs

Wood Walkway, See Sheet L4.04

③ L5.01 Sloped Green Roof System - 6" Soil Depth

South Wave
See Sheet L3.02

Metal Grating
See Sheet L4.02

North Wave
See Sheet L3.01

Wood Deck Walkway, See Sheet L4.04

NOTE:
These Sections are for Reference Only to show Relative Relationships between Site Elements. Refer to Details as noted.

147

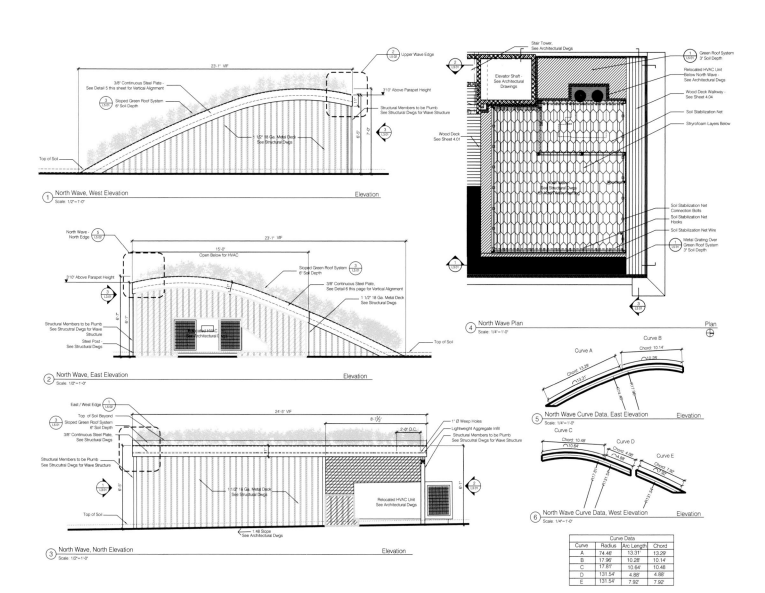

① North Wave, West Elevation
Scale: 1/2"=1'-0"   Elevation

② North Wave, East Elevation
Scale: 1/2"=1'-0"   Elevation

③ North Wave, North Elevation
Scale: 1/2"=1'-0"   Elevation

④ North Wave Plan
Scale: 1/4"=1'-0"   Plan

⑤ North Wave Curve Data, East Elevation
Scale: 1/4"=1'-0"   Elevation

⑥ North Wave Curve Data, West Elevation
Scale: 1/4"=1'-0"   Elevation

Curve Data			
Curve	Radius	Arc Length	Chord
A	74.46'	13.31'	13.29'
B	17.96'	10.28'	10.14'
C	17.81'	10.64'	10.48'
D	131.54'	4.88'	4.88'
E	131.54'	7.92'	7.92'

148

SOUTH WAVE ELEVATION (L3.02)

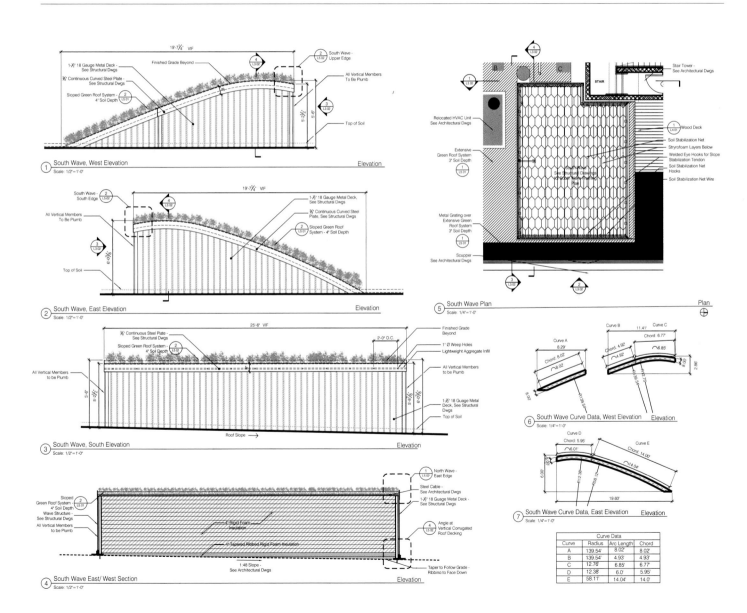

① South Wave, West Elevation
Scale: 1/2"=1'-0"

② South Wave, East Elevation
Scale: 1/2"=1'-0"

③ South Wave, South Elevation
Scale: 1/2"=1'-0"

④ South Wave East/West Section
Scale: 1/2"=1'-0"

⑤ South Wave Plan
Scale: 1/4"=1'-0"

⑥ South Wave Curve Data, West Elevation
Scale: 1/4"=1'-0"

⑦ South Wave Curve Data, East Elevation
Scale: 1/4"=1'-0"

Curve Data			
Curve	Radius	Arc Length	Chord
A	139.54'	8.02'	8.02'
B	139.54'	4.93'	4.93'
C	12.76'	6.85'	6.77'
D	12.38'	6.0'	5.95'
E	58.11'	14.04'	14.0'

WOOD WALKWAY (L4.04)

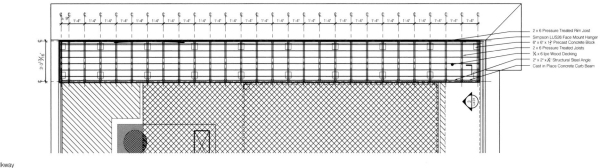

2 x 6 Pressure Treated Rim Joist
Simpson LUS26 Face Mount Hanger
6" x 6" x 1½" Precast Concrete Block
2 x 6 Pressure Treated Joists
⅞ x 6 Ipe Wood Decking
2" x 2" x ⅜" Structural Steel Angle
Cast in Place Concrete Curb Beam

① Wood Walkway   Plan
  Scale: 1/2"=1'-0"

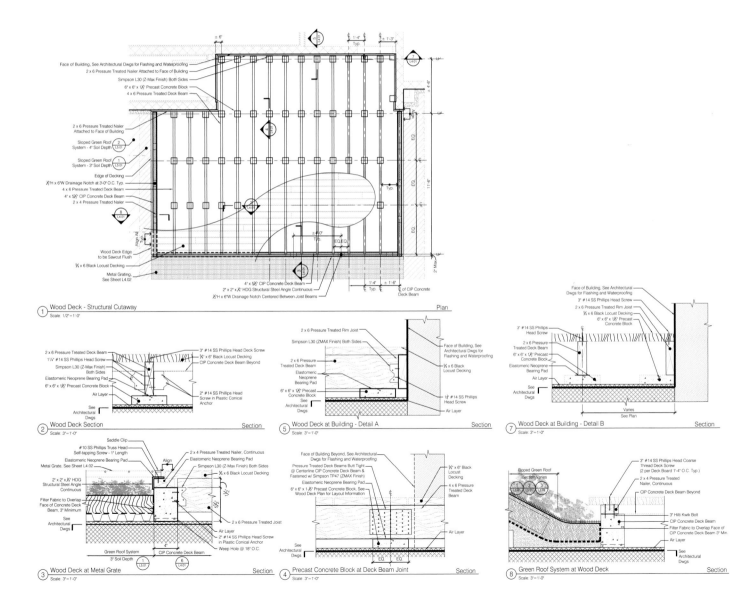

1 Wood Deck - Structural Cutaway
Scale: 1/2"= 1'-0"

2 Wood Deck Section
Scale: 3"= 1'-0"

3 Wood Deck at Metal Grate
Scale: 3"= 1'-0"

4 Precast Concrete Block at Deck Beam Joint
Scale: 3"= 1'-0"

5 Wood Deck at Building - Detail A
Scale: 3"= 1'-0"

7 Wood Deck at Building - Detail B
Scale: 3"= 1'-0"

8 Green Roof System at Wood Deck
Scale: 3"= 1'-0"

151

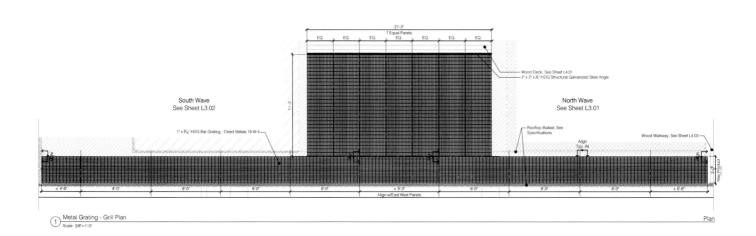

1 Metal Grating - Grill Plan
Scale: 3/8"=1'-0"

Plan

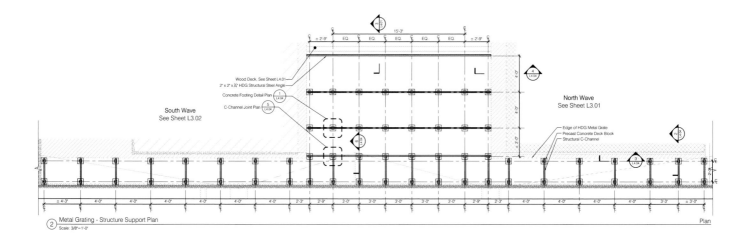

2 Metal Grating - Structure Support Plan
Scale: 3/8"=1'-0"

Plan

METAL GRATING DETAILS (L4.04)

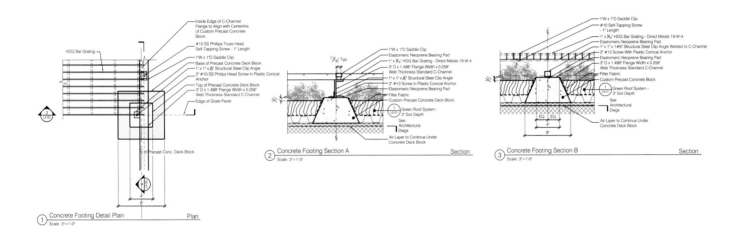

1 Concrete Footing Detail Plan — Plan
Scale: 3"=1'-0"

HCG Bar Grating

Inside Edge of C-Channel Flange to Align with Centerline of Custom Precast Concrete Block
#10 SS Phillips Truss Head Self-Tapping Screw - 1" Length
1"W x 1"D Saddle Clip
Base of Precast Concrete Deck Block
1" x 1" x ⅛" Structural Steel Clip Angle
2" #10 SS Philips Head Screw in Plastic Conical Anchor
Top of Precast Concrete Deck Block
3" D x 1.498" Flange Width x 0.258" Web Thickness Standard C-Channel
Edge of Grate Panel

CL of Precast Conc. Deck Block

2 Concrete Footing Section A — Section
Scale: 3"=1'-0"

1"W x 1"D Saddle Clip
Elastomeric Neoprene Bearing Pad
1" x ⁷⁄₁₆" HDG Bar Grating - Direct Metals 19-W-4
3" D x 1.498" Flange Width x 0.258" Web Thickness Standard C-Channel
1" x 1" x ⅛" Structural Steel Clip Angle
1" x ⅛" Structural Steel Clip Angle
2" #10 Screw in Plastic Conical Anchor
Elastomeric Neoprene Bearing Pad
Filter Fabric
Custom Precast Concrete Deck Block
Green Roof System - 3" Soil Depth
See Architectural Dwgs
Air Layer to Continue Under Concrete Deck Block

3 Concrete Footing Section B — Section
Scale: 3"=1'-0"

1"W x 1"D Saddle Clip
#10 Self-Tapping Screw - 1" Length
1" x ⁷⁄₁₆" HDG Bar Grating - Direct Metals 19-W-4
Elastomeric Neoprene Bearing Pad
1" x 1" x 1#8" Structural Steel Clip Angle Welded to C-Channel
2" #10 Screw With Plastic Conical Anchor
Elastomeric Neoprene Bearing Pad
3" D x 1.498" Flange Width x 0.258" Web Thickness Standard C-Channel
Filter Fabric
Custom Precast Concrete Block
Green Roof System - 3" Soil Depth
Air Layer to Continue Under Concrete Deck Block

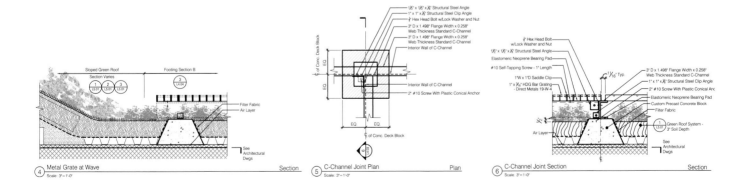

4 Metal Grate at Wave — Section
Scale: 3"=1'-0"

Sloped Green Roof Section Varies
Footing Section B
Filter Fabric
Air Layer
See Architectural Dwgs

5 C-Channel Joint Plan — Plan
Scale: 3"=1'-0"

½" x 1½" x ¼" Structural Steel Clip Angle
1" x 1" x ¼" Structural Steel Clip Angle
¼" Hex Head Bolt w/Lock Washer and Nut
3" D x 1.498" Flange Width x 0.258" Web Thickness Standard C-Channel
3" D x 1.498" Flange Width x 0.258" Web Thickness Standard C-Channel
Interior Wall of C-Channel
Interior Wall of C-Channel
2" #10 Screw With Plastic Conical Anchor

CL of Conc. Deck Block

6 C-Channel Joint Section — Section
Scale: 3"=1'-0"

¼" Hex Head Bolt w/Lock Washer and Nut
½" x 1½" x ¼" Structural Steel Clip Angle
Elastomeric Neoprene Bearing Pad
#10 Self-Tapping Screw - 1" Length
1"W x 1"D Saddle Clip
1" x ⁷⁄₁₆" HDG Bar Grating - Direct Metals 19-W-4
3" D x 1.498" Flange Width x 0.258" Web Thickness Standard C-Channel
1" x 1" x ¼" Structural Steel Clip Angle
Elastomeric Neoprene Bearing Pad
Custom Precast Concrete Block
Filter Fabric
Green Roof System - 3" Soil Depth
See Architectural Dwgs
Air Layer

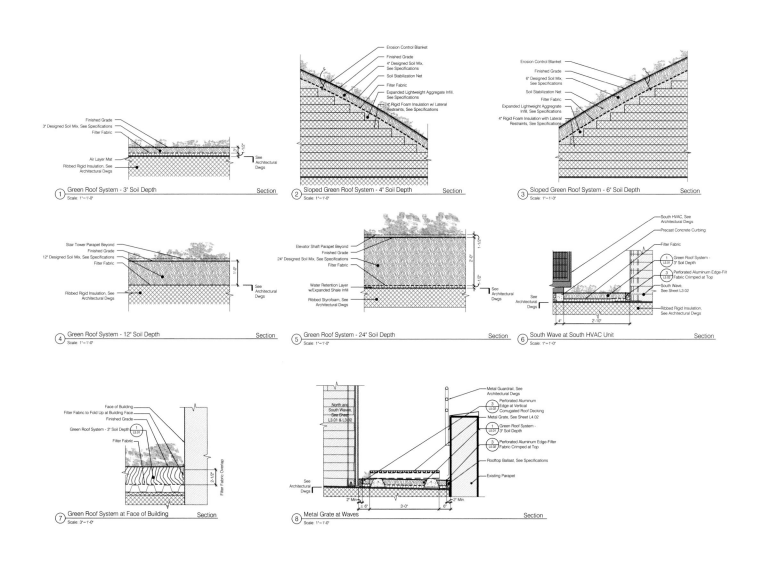

1 Green Roof System - 3" Soil Depth — Section
Scale: 1"=1'-0"

2 Sloped Green Roof System - 4" Soil Depth — Section
Scale: 1"=1'-0"

3 Sloped Green Roof System - 6" Soil Depth — Section
Scale: 1"=1'-0"

4 Green Roof System - 12" Soil Depth — Section
Scale: 1"=1'-0"

5 Green Roof System - 24" Soil Depth — Section
Scale: 1"=1'-0"

6 South Wave at South HVAC Unit — Section
Scale: 1"=1'-0"

7 Green Roof System at Face of Building — Section
Scale: 3"=1'-0"

8 Metal Grate at Waves — Section
Scale: 1"=1'-0"

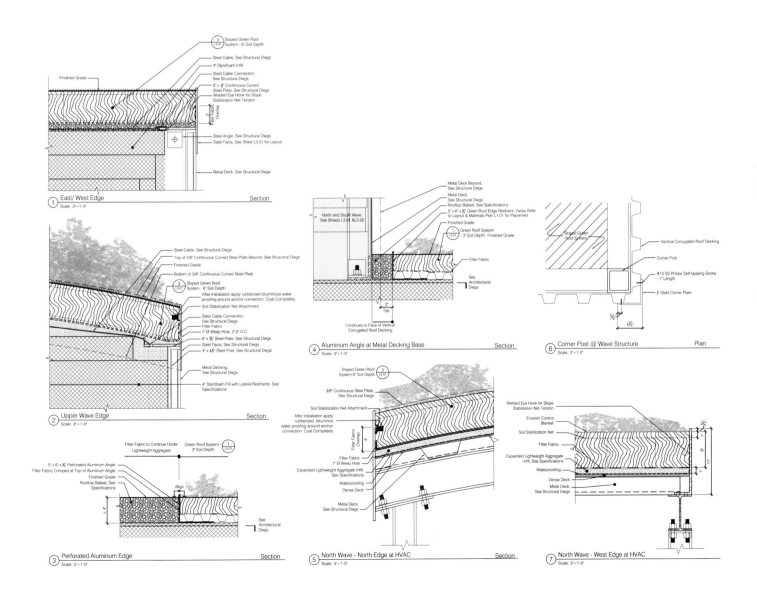

1. East/West Edge — Section
   Scale: 3"=1'-0"

2. Upper Wave Edge — Section
   Scale: 3"=1'-0"

3. Perforated Aluminum Edge — Section
   Scale: 3"=1'-0"

4. Aluminum Angle at Metal Decking Base — Section
   Scale: 3"=1'-0"

5. North Wave - North Edge at HVAC — Section
   Scale: 3"=1'-0"

6. Corner Post @ Wave Structure — Plan
   Scale: 3"=1'-0"

7. North Wave - West Edge at HVAC
   Scale: 3"=1'-0"

ACKNOWLEDGMENTS

This book would not exist without the help of numerous people and agencies. Foremost, I want to thank Michael Van Valkenburgh, who encouraged my research on green infrastructure in the United States, and who opened his office for my inquiries. After I made the American Society of Landscape Architects roof my main case study, Chris Counts and John Gidding from Michael Van Valkenburgh Associates provided me with a constant flow of critical information that enabled me to gain in-depth understanding of the project. Without their incredible engagement and tireless support throughout this entire process, the description and depiction of the ASLA roof would not have been possible.

I also want to thank all the persons I interviewed and who shared important knowledge with me during my ASLA roof research: Nancy Somerville, Dennis Carmichael and Gerald Beaulieu from ASLA, Marcus de la fleur and David Yocca from Conservation Design Forum, Jeannette Laramee, the resourceful structural engineer from Silman Associates, and two excellent plant specialists, Richard Hindle of MVVA and Ed Snodgrass.

Without a strong set of ideas, the existence of a book is unjustifiable. It should be noted that my request for a socially responsive green infrastructure in our cities could not stand without the ideas and works of a generation of practitioners before me, namely my exposure to the work of the landscape architecture firm Latz + Partners whose combination of environmental research with landscape theory and design is a continuing source of inspiration to me.

I not only want to thank Peter Latz for the insight he has given me into the early beginnings of his green roof research but also all the other German green roof pioneers; Hans-Joachim Liesecke, Bernd Krupka, and Reinhard Bornkamm who submitted to comprehensive interviews. Special thanks go to the green roof specialists Katrin Scholz-Barth, Wigbert Riehl, Fritz Häemmerle, Manfred Köhler, and Stephan Brenneisen, who made many helpful comments, answered questions, read and commented on parts of the manuscript, and freely shared detailed information with me. Several more planning professionals closely examined my essay and helped improve it. For this I owe gratitude to my colleagues Holly Getch Clarke, Wolfram Hoefer, Hans-Joachim Liesecke, and Nigel Dunnett.

The content of the book would not be the same without the help of a group of people who reviewed the literature, acquired the image rights, composed maps and collages, and visited various roof tops in dizzying heights. Foremost, I want to thank my dear colleague and friend Guido Mertes for his scouting and detective work on German soil. He was my foreign correspondent and laid the groundwork. On the American side, I want to thank my committed research assistants, Graduate School of Design students, who all brought a special gift to the project: Jennifer Wai-Kwun Toy, Joshua Haddad, and Beatrice Saraga.

I could not have compensated them for their time without a grant from the Graduate School of Design administered by Margaret Crawford, Carl Steinitz, Dan Schodek, and Dean Alan Altshuler. I not only want to thank those individuals and the school for financially jumpstarting my research but also for giving important advice and guidance. Their seed funding was amended by a grant from the ASLA covering travel expenses within the United States, and by a grant from the Tozier Fund covering graphic exploration. For both I am very grateful.

Many thanks go to Princeton Architectural Press and its editors who supported me through various phases: Nancy Eklund-Later, Clare Jacobson and Sara Hart who copyedited the first version, and Jennifer Thompson who not only finalized all edits but was also instrumental in the final appearance and structure of the book. Special thanks go to the graphic designer Paul Wagner who merged text and image to create such a clear and elegant product.

Finally, I want to thank the numerous building managers and janitors of all the buildings I visited; they walked countless flights of stairs with me, crossed through crowded maintenance rooms, ducked under air vents, climbed ladders, opened hatches and escape doors in order to let me enter roof spaces that otherwise only belonged to them.

PROJECT CREDITS

CLIENT
American Society of Landscape Architects

GREEN ROOF TASK FORCE
J. Kipp Shrack, FASLA, Chair
Dennis B. Carmichael, FASLA
Barbara L. Deutsch, ASLA
Bruce D. Dvorak, ASLA
Jeff S. Lee, ASLA
Susan L. B. Jacobson, FASLA
Patrick A. Miller, FASLA
Gerald P. Beaulieu
Nancy C. Somerville

LEAD DESIGNER AND PRIME CONSULTANT, LANDSCAPE ARCHITECT
Michael Van Valkenburgh Associates, Inc. (MVVA)
Michael Van Valkenburgh, FASLA—Principal in charge
Chris Counts, ASLA—Project manager and designer
Stephen Noone, ASLA—Associate in charge of construction
John Gidding—Junior designer
Robert Rock—Design staff
Richard Hindle—Monitoring program

CONSULTING LANDSCAPE ARCHITECT
Conservation Design Forum (CDF)
David Yocca, ASLA—Principal in charge
Marcus de la fleur, ASLA—Project manager and designer

ARCHITECT
DMJM Design/AECOM
David A. Daileda, FAIA—Principal in charge
Brandi Wallis—Project designer
Ali Jannati—Project HVAC designer

ENGINEER
Robert Silman Associates, PC
Kirk Mettam—Principal in charge
Jeannette Laramee—Project manager and designer

CONSULTING GREEN ROOF MANUFACTURER
American Hydrotech, Inc.
Steve Skinner

CONSULTING NURSERY
Emory Knoll Farms, Inc.
Ed Snodgrass

PRODUCTS AND SERVICE SPONSORS
Emory Knoll Farms, Inc. / Greenroofplants.com—Green roof plants and consulting services
American Hydrotech, Inc.—Green roof assembly
Green Roof Products / St. Louis Metal Works—Edging and drains
Ohio Gratings—Grating for walking surface
Outdoor Illumination—Lighting design
ForestWorld Group—Ipe wood for decking
Dow Chemical—Extruded polystyrene insulation
Rain Bird—Drip Division: Drip irrigation system
Outside Unlimited—Installation of drip irrigation system
Carolina Stalite Company—Green roof media

BIBLIOGRAPHY

Atelier 5. *Atelier 5: Siedlungen und städtebauliche Projekte.* Braunschweig, Germany: Vieweg, 1994.

Betsky, Aaron. *Landscrapers: Building with the Land.* New York: Thames & Hudson, 2002.

Bornkamm, Reinhard. "Vegetation und Vegetationsentwicklung auf Kiesdächern." *Vegetatio* (Germany) no. 10 (1961): 1–23.

———. "Untersuchungen zur kostensparenden Begrünung von Dachflächen." *Das Gartenamt* (Germany) no. 3 (1977).

———. "Dachvegetation und Dachbegrünung." *Landschaftsentwicklung und Umweltforschung* (Germany) no. 76 (1990): 4–13.

Brenneisen, Stephan. "Biodiversity of European Greenroofs." Paper submitted for Greening Rooftops for Sustainable Communities conference. Chicago, 2003.

———. "Green Roofs: Recapturing Urban Space for Wildlife: a Challenge for Urban Planning and Environmental Education." Paper submitted for Greening Rooftops for Sustainable Communities conference. Washington DC, 2005.

Coffman, Reid, and Graham Davis. "Insect and Avian Fauna Presence on the Ford Assembly Plant Ecoroof." Paper submitted for Greening Rooftops for Sustainable Communities conference. Washington DC, 2005.

Dunnett, Nigel, and James Hitchmough. *The Dynamic Landscape.* London: Spon Press, 2004.

Dunnett, Nigel, and Noël Kingsbury. *Planting Green Roofs and Living Walls.* Portland, Oreg.: Timber Press, 2004.

Earth Pledge. *Green Roof: Ecological Design and Construction.* Atglen, Pa.: Schiffer Publishing, 2005.

Evans, Ronald L. *A Gardener's Guide to Sedums.* London: The Alpine Garden Society, n.d.

Flora, Paul. *Penthouse.* New York: Harry N. Abrams, 1978.

Forschungsgesellschaft Landschaftsentwicklung Landschaftsbau e.V. *Guideline for the Planning, Execution and Upkeep of Green-Roof Sites.* Bonn, Germany: FLL, 2002.

Frampton, Kenneth. "Die Entwicklung des modernen Siedlungsbaus und der Beitrag von Atelier 5." In *Atelier 5: Siedlungen und städtebauliche Projekte*, 12–21. Braunschweig, Germany: Vieweg, 1994.

Gedge, Dusty, and Mathew Frith. "An Eye for the Green Top: an Independent Voice for Green Roofs in the UK." Paper submitted for Greening Rooftops for Sustainable Communities conference. Washington DC, 2005.

Gollwitzer, Gerda, and Werner Wirsing. *Dachflächen: Bewohnt, belebt, bepflanzt.* München, Germany: Georg D.W. Callwey, 1971.

Hämmerle, Fritz. *Der Gründachmarkt leidet unter Wachstumshemmern* (2005). http://www.haemmerle-gruendach.de/marktspiegel.html.

Händeler, Erik. *Die Geschichte der Zukunft.* Moers, Germany: Brendow Verlag, 2003.

Henze, Anton, and Bernhard Moosbrugger. *La Tourette: Le Corbusier's erster Klosterbau.* Starnberg, Germany: Josef Keller Verlag, 1993.

Kähler, Gert. "Roofscapes." *Daidalos* no. 42 (1991): 122–29.

Kephart, Paul. "Living Architecture—an Ecological Approach." Paper submitted for Greening Rooftops for Sustainable Communities conference. Washington DC, 2005.

Köhler, Manfred, and Melissa Keeley. "Berlin, Green Roof Technology and Policy Development." In *Green Roofs: Ecological Design and Construction*, 108–12. Atglen, Pa.: Schiffer Publishing, 2005.

Krupka, Bernd. *Dachbegrünung.* Stuttgart, Germany: Ulmer, 1992.

———. "Entwicklung und Bedeutung der Dachbegrünung." In *Beiträge zur räumlichen Planung*, vol. 57, 285–304. Hannover: Fachbereich Landschaftsarchitektur und Umweltentwicklung der Universität Hannover, 2001.

Landolt, Elias. "Orchideen-Wiesen in Wollishofen (Zürich): ein erstaunliches Relikt aus dem Anfang des 20. Jahrhunderts." *Vierteljahresschrift der Naturforschenden Gesellschaft in Zürich* (Zürich) (2001) 146/2–3, 41–51.

Le Corbusier. "The Conquest of the Flat Roof." In *Das Neue Frankfurt, Monatsschrift für die Fragen der Grosstadtgestaltung* 7. Frankfurt, Germany: Englert und Schlosser, 1927, 167–69.

———. *Une petite maison.* Zürich: Aux Editions d'architecture, 1954.

Le Corbusier & P. Jeanneret. *Oeuvre Complete 1934–1938.* 4th ed. Zürich: Girsberger, 1951.

Le Roy, Louis G. *Natur ausschalten-Natur einschalten*. Stuttgart, Germany: Klett-Cotta, 1983.

Liesecke, Hans-Joachim. "Entstehung und Entwicklung der extensiven Dachbegrünung." In *Dach+Grün*, no. 4. Stuttgart: 2005.

———. "Vegetationstechnische Gesichtspunkte bei der Begrünung von Flachdächern." In *Deutscher Gartenbau* no. 29 (1975): 1223–26.

Lundholm, Jeremy. "A Habitat Temple Approach to Green Building Surfaces." Paper submitted for Greening Rooftops for Sustainable Communities conference. Washington DC, 2005.

Maasz, Harry. "Der Garten auf dem Dach." In *Meyer-Ries: Gartentechnik und Gartenkunst*, 518–21. Nordhausen, Germany: Heinrich Killinger Verlagsgesellschaft, 1930.

Martínez, Andrés. *Dwelling on the Roof*. Barcelona, Spain: Editorial Gustavo Gili, 2005.

May, Ernst. "Das flache Dach." In *Das Neue Frankfurt, Monatsschrift für die Fragen der Grosstadtgestaltung*, 199–52. Frankfurt, Germany: Englert und Schlosser, 1927.

Migge, Leberecht. "Das grüne Dach." In *Das Neue Frankfurt, Monatsschrift für die Fragen der Grosstadtgestaltung* 7, 182. Frankfurt, Germany: Englert und Schlosser, 1927.

Neumann, Klaus. "Grüne Dächer als Herausforderung für die Zukunft." In *International Green Roof Congress, 2004 Nürtingen*. Berlin, Germany: International Green Roof Association, 2004.

Osmundsen, Theodore. *Roof Gardens: History Design and Construction*. New York: W.W. Norton, 1999.

Potie, Philippe. *Le Corbusier: The Monastery of Sainte de La Tourette*. Basel, Switzerland: Birkhäuser, 2001.

Riehl, Wigbert. "Regelwerke, Techniken, Bauweisen: Grundlagen zur Dachbegrünung." In *Garten + Landschaft* 10, 36–38. München, Germany: Callwey, 2003.

Rowe, Bradley. "Evaluation of Sedum and Michigan Native Taxa for Green Roof Applications." Paper submitted for Greening Rooftops for Sustainable Communities conference. Washington DC, 2005.

Rüber, Eduard. *Das Rasendach, die wohlfeilste, dauerhafteste und feuersicherste Eindeckungsart*. Hannover, Germany: Schäfer, 2002.

Scholz-Barth, Katrin, and Ed Snodgrass. "Green Roof Materials and Components." In *Green Roofs, Ecological Design and Construction*, ed. Earth Pledge, 134–36. Atglen, Pa.: Schiffer Publishing, 2005.

Snodgrass, Ed. "100 Extensive Green Roofs: Lessons Learned." Paper submitted for Greening Rooftops for Sustainable Communities conference. Washington DC, 2005.

Stifter, Roland. *Dachgärten: Grüne Inseln in der Stadt*. Stuttgart, Germany: Ulmer Verlag, 1988.

Wolschke-Buhlmann, Joachim. "Anmerkungen zur historischen Entwicklung von Dachgärten im frühen 20. Jahrhundert." In *Beiträge zur räumlichen Planung*, 271–83. Vol. 2. Hannover, Germany: Fachbereich Landschaftsarchitektur und Umweltentwicklung der Universität Hannover, 2001.

IMAGE CREDITS